Anonymous

The River Hudson

Together with descriptions and illustrations of the city of New York, Catskill Mountains, Lake George, Lake Champlain, Saratoga. Illustrated with fifty engravings.

Anonymous

The River Hudson

Together with descriptions and illustrations of the city of New York, Catskill Mountains, Lake George, Lake Champlain, Saratoga. Illustrated with fifty engravings.

ISBN/EAN: 9783337301545

Printed in Europe, USA, Canada, Australia, Japan

Cover: Foto ©Andreas Hilbeck / pixelio.de

More available books at **www.hansebooks.com**

THE STEAMBOAT & RAILROAD TRAVELLER'S GUIDE TO THE HUDSON RIVER,

WITH DESCRIPTIONS AND ILLUSTRATIONS OF

ITS SUBLIME SCENERY

AND

PLACES OF INTEREST

ALONG THE ROUTE,

AS WELL AS OF

THE SHAKER SETTLEMENT, THE CATSKILL MOUNTAINS,

LAKE GEORGE, SARATOGA,

AND

THE CITY OF NEW YORK.

PROFUSELY ILLUSTRATED WITH ENGRAVINGS

From Photographs and Pencil Drawings.

NEW YORK:

ALEX. HARTHILL AND COMPANY,

20 NORTH WILLIAM STREET.

Sold by Booksellers and News Agents everywhere.

PRICE TWENTY-FIVE CENTS.

STEINWAY & SONS'

Patent Overstrung

GRAND &  **SQUARE**

PIANO-FORTES,

ARE NOW CONSIDERED THE BEST PIANOS MANUFACTURED.

THESE PIANOS HAVE TAKEN THE FIRST PREMIUM,

Where and whenever Exhibited in Competition with the Best Makers of

NEW YORK, BOSTON, PHILADELPHIA AND BALTIMORE.

AMONG THE JUDGES WERE

GOTTSCHALK, WM. MASON, H. A. WOLLENHAUPT,

AND OTHER MUSICAL CELEBRITIES.

CERTIFICATE given by nearly all our Greatest and most Prominent Musicians and Artists regarding our Instruments:

NEW-YORK, JAN. 1860.

The undersigned, having personally examined and practically tested the improvement in Grand Pianos, invented by H. STEINWAY, in which the covered strings are overstrung above those remaining, do hereby certify:

1. That as a result of the said Improvement the voice of the Piano is greatly improved in quality and power.

2. The sound by Steinway's Improvement is much more even, less harsh, stronger, and much better prolonged, than that realized in any other Piano with which we are acquainted.

3. The undersigned regard the improvement of Mr. Steinway as most novel, ingenious and important. No Piano of similar construction has ever been known or used, so far as the undesigned know or believe.

GUSTAV SATTER, WILLIAM MASON, S. B. MILLS, JOHN N. PATTISON.
WM. SAAR, ROBERT GOLDBECK, U. C. HILL, GEORGE W. MORGAN,
WM. A. KING, CARL BERGMANN, GEO. F. BRISTOW, HENRY C. TIMM,
AND MANY OTHERS.

Every Instrument Warranted for the Term of Five Years.

Ware Rooms, Nos. 82 & 84 Walker Street, near Broadway,

NEW YORK.

CHILSON'S CONE FURNACE,

Patented in America, England and France.

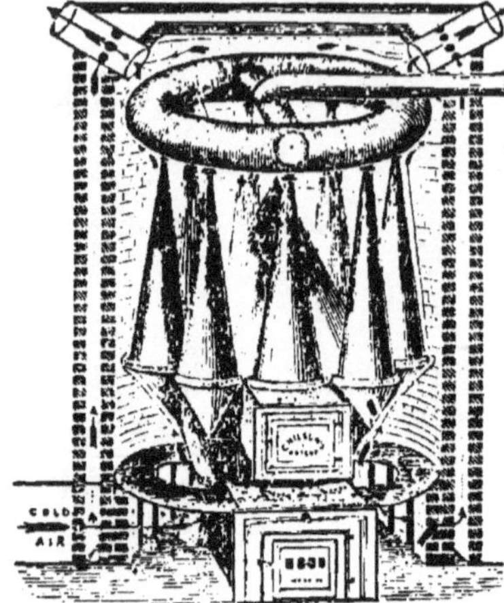

The subscriber's long experience in the invention, manufacture and erection of FURNACES, enables him with confidence to publicly challenge all other known inventions for heating buildings to equal the "CONE FURNACE" in any particular, as more than *twenty-five hundred testimonials*, received during the last five years, will prove. Every intelligent person will at once comprehend, by an examination of the engraving, the peculiar advantages combined in this Furnace, with its broad, shallow fire-pot, its cluster of tapering radiators or cones standing over the fire, holding the smoke and gas back near the fire, and thereby causing a thorough and perfect combustion, while the heat is made to impinge against and radiate from the immense cone surfaces, thus combining a powerful heater with great economy in fuel, superior strength and durability of the apparatus (with no joints over the fire to allow leakage of gas or smoke,) simplicity of structure, ease of management, and above all, a fresh, healthful heat, free from the scorching, disagreeable odors common to the usual Hot-Air Furnaces, (emitted from their red-hot cylinders, cracked pots, and broken joints.)

The "CONE" received a GOLD MEDAL at the last Fair in Boston, and the only Gold Medal ever awarded to a Furnace in Massachusetts.

CHILSON'S ELEVATED
DOUBLE OVEN COOKING RANGE.

No Housekeeper Should Fail to Examine It.

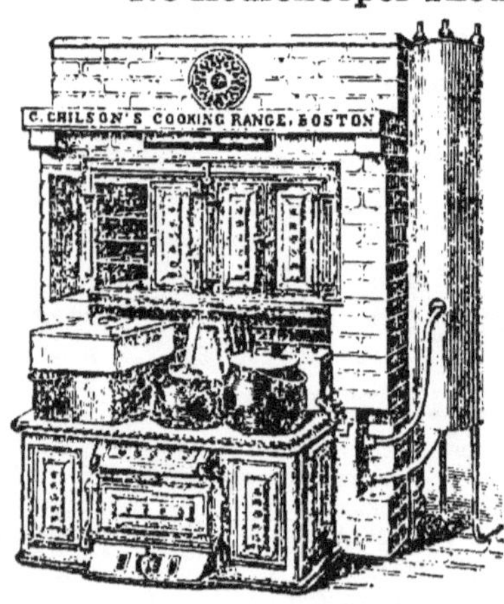

The highly satisfactory testimony received from the large number of these Ranges in use, makes it quite certain that no housekeeper will long use any other plan of Cooking Range or Stove after once seeing this Range. And feeling confident that it must come into general use, it was determined it should be got up so very perfect in its principle and workmanship, as to have no equal in the world—and a visit to my store in Boston, or my foundry at Mansfield, will prove the truthfulness of this assertion, and show the largest and much the best assortment of Ranges and Furnaces to be found in any one establishment in the United States. This Range excels all others in its entirely new principle and thorough workmanship, its extra, heavy fine castings, its great economy in the use of fuel, and in its own cost, its quick and even baking ovens, its simplicity and ease of management, its self-regulating flues, avoiding the usual vexatious complication of dampers, and its flue plates, preventing the loss of heat in the brick walls.

These last two improvements will open the eyes of the Economist, to see how great is the saving in fuel over the extravagant waste in other ranges. Sizes in variety for dwellings, hotels, &c., with or without Water Backs. Hot-Air Fixtures for heating additional rooms, Hot Closets, &c.

WITH A FULL ASSORTMENT OF

MANTELS, GRATES, REGISTERS, VENTILATORS,
STOVES, &c.

AT WHOLESALE AND RETAIL.

Personal attention given to the erection of Heating, Cooking and Ventilating Apparatus in any part of the country.

Ware Rooms, 99 & 101 Blackstone Street, Boston,

FOUNDRY AT MANSFIELD, MASS.

GARDNER CHILSON.

THE

RIVER HUDSON,

TOGETHER WITH

Descriptions and Illustrations

OF

THE CITY OF NEW YORK,

CATSKILL MOUNTAINS, LAKE CHAMPLAIN,

LAKE GEORGE, SARATOGA.

ILLUSTRATED WITH FIFTY ENGRAVINGS

NEW YORK:
ALEX. HARTHILL AND COMPANY,
20 NORTH WILLIAM STREET.
Sold by Booksellers and News Agents everywhere.

PATENT WIRE FENCING.

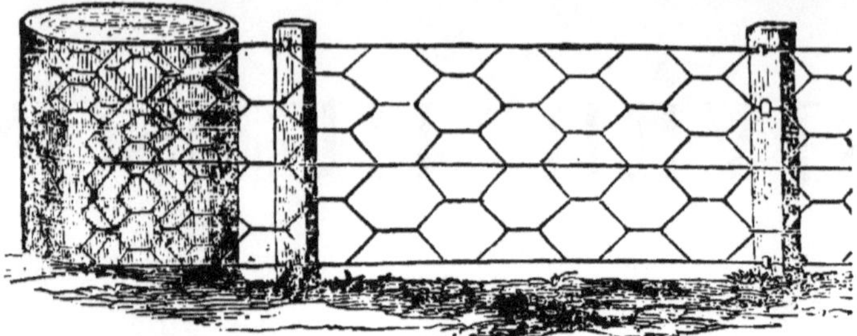

The above cut represents **PATENT WIRE FENCING**, manufactured of Annealed Wire, and likewise Galvanized Annealed Wire, of Various kinds, adapted to Field, Railroad, and Ornamental purposes. Prices ranging from 75 cents to $3 per rod. Descriptive Catalogues may be had gratis by applying to

Z. HOSMER & CO., 33 Batterymarch Street, Boston, Mass.

COUGHS, COLDS, HOARSENESS

AND

BROWN'S BRONCHIAL TROCHES

INFLUENZA, IRRITATION, SORENESS, or any affection of the Throat CURED, the HACKING COUGH in CONSUMPTION, BRONCHITIS, WHOOPING COUGH, ASTHMA, CATARRH, RELIEVED by BROWN'S BRONCHIAL TROCHES or COUGH LOZENGES.

"A simple and elegant combination for Coughs, &c."—Dr. G. F. BIGELOW, Boston.

"Have proved extremely serviceable for Hoarseness."—Rev. HENRY WARD BEECHER.

"I recommend their use to Public Speakers."—Rev. E. H. CHAPIN, New York.

"That trouble in my throat, (for which the 'Troches' is a specific) having made me often a mere whisperer."—N. P. WILLIS.

"Most salutary relief in Bronchitis."—Rev. S. SEIGFRIED, Morristown, Ohio.

"Beneficial when compelled to speak, suffering from cold."—Rev. S. J. P. ANDERSON, St. Louis.

"Effectual in removing Hoarseness and Irritation of the Throat, so common with speakers and singers."—Prof. M. STACY JOHNSON, La Grange, Ga., Teacher of Music in Southern Female College.

"Great benefit when taken before and after preaching, as they prevent Hoarseness. From their past effect, I think they will be of permanent advantage to me."—Rev. E. ROWLEY, A. M. President Athens College, Tenn.

Sold by all Druggists at 25 cents per box.

Also, BROWN'S LAXATIVE TROCHES, or Cathartic Lozenges, for Dyspepsia, Indigestion, Constipation, Headache, Bilious Affections, &c.

"GET THE BEST."

WEBSTER'S UNABRIDGED DICTIONARY.

NEW PICTORIAL EDITION.

1500 *Pictorial Illustrations.*

9000 to 10,000 NEW WORDS in the Vocabulary. Table of SYNONYMS, by Prof Goodrich. Table giving Pronunciation of the names of 8000 distinguished psrsons of Modern Times. Peculiar use of words and Terms in the Bible. With other new features, together with all the matter of previous edtions.

In One Volume of 1750 Pages. Price $6.50. Sold by all Booksellers.

"GET THE BEST." "GET THE BEST."

C. & G. MERRIAM, Springfield, Mass.

CONTENTS.

CONTENTS.

LIST OF ILLUSTRATIONS.

HUDSON RIVER FROM THE RAILROAD.

Although our description of the scenic beauties of the Hudson River is taken from the deck of an upward bound steamer, it by no means follows that the flying passenger on the Hudson River Railway may not, partially at least, enjoy the trip with us. As the cars make a brief stop at each of the places on the east side of the river which we have named, the passenger may, by keeping our description in view, know at what place, at what time, and in what direction to turn his eye in order to witness the different objects of interest we have endeavoured to portray. As the cars run close to the water's edge along the entire route from New York to Albany, the passenger can at all times command a full view of the river, as well as of the towns and villages lying on the western bank, and also of the Palisades and Catskill Mountains. For the benefit of our railway readers we append a list of the towns lying on the railroad—in their regular order—together with a few of the places situated opposite each station, with distances from town to town, and from New York.

From New York to Albany.

NEW YORK.	*Miles.*	*From N.Y.*	*Opposite.*	*Objects of Interest.*
Manhattan....	8	....	Bull's Ferry	.... Forts Lee and Washington.
Yonkers	9	17	Palisades	.... Fonthill, E. Forrest.
Dobb's Ferry..	6	23	Piermont	.... Washington's Head-quarters.
Tarrytown....	5	28	Nyack	.... Andre's place of arrest.
Sing Sing.....	5	33 ...	Rockland Lake	.... State Prison.
Peekskill	11	44	Caldwell's Landing	.... Highlands.
Garrisons.....	8	52	West Point	.... Military Academy, and views.
Cold Spring ..	3	55	Canterbury	.... Cronest and Storm King.
Fishkill	6	61	Newbury	.... Idlewild, N.P. Willis'; Turk's Face.
Hamburg.....	6	67	Hampton	.... Scenery.
Poughkeepsie..	9	76	New Paltz	.... "
Hyde Park ...	6	82	————	.... J. K. Paulding's residence.
Staatsburg. ..	5	87	Pelham	.... Scenery.
Rhinebeck....	6	93	Rondout	.... Rondout Creek.
Barrytown ...	5	98	Glasgow	.... Scenery.
Tivoli	4	102	Saugerties	.... "
Germantown..	5	107	Malden	.... Catskill Mountains.
Oakhill	5	112	Catskill	.... Mountain House, &c.
Hudson	6	118	Athens	.... Catskill Mountains.
Stockport	4	122	————	... Scenery.
Stuyvesant ...	3	125	Coxsackie	.... "
Kinderhook Sta.	3	128	————	.... Birth-place of M. Van Buren.
Schodac	7	135	New Baltimore	.... Scenery.
Castleton	3	138	Coeyman's	.... "
East Albany ..	6	144	Albany	.... "
Troy	8	152	West Troy	.... City.

Total distance from New York to Albany, 144 miles: to Troy, 152.

CHART OF THE RIVER HUDSON WITH DISTANCES

BETWEEN NEW YORK AND TROY.

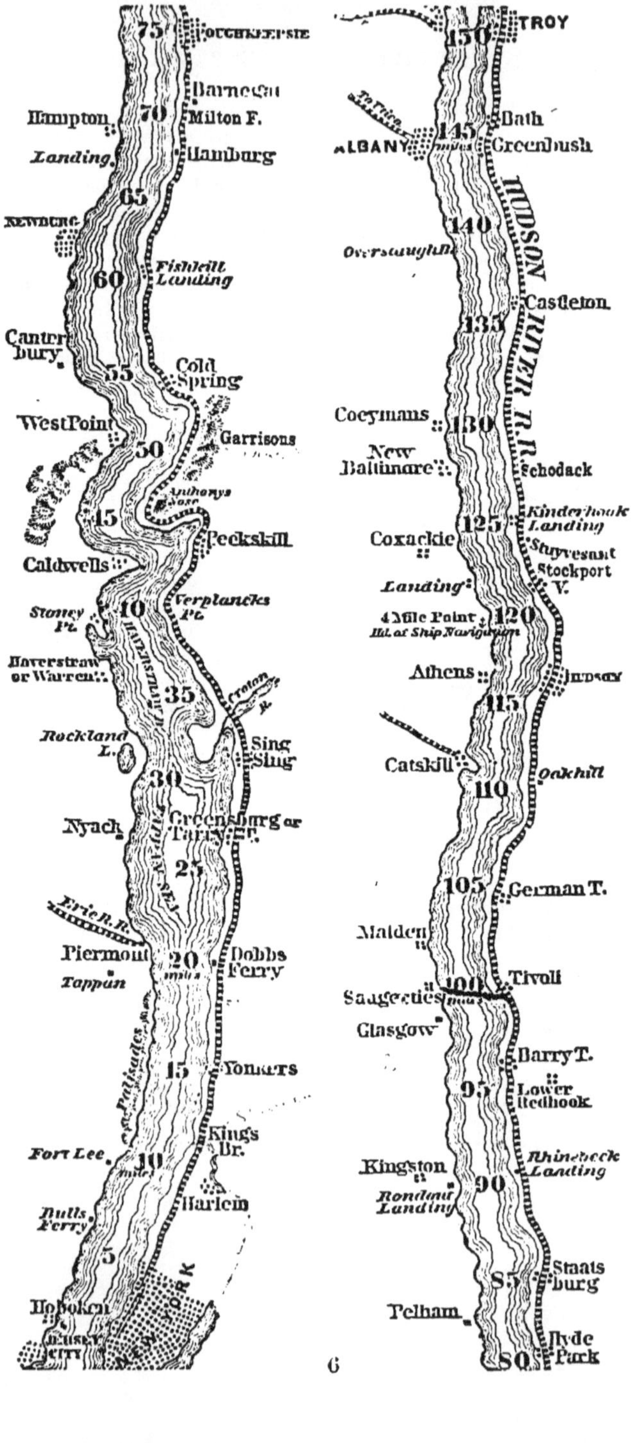

Poughkeepsie
Barnegat
Hampton Landing
Milton F.
Hamburg
Newburg
Fishkill Landing
Canterbury
Cold Spring
West Point
Garrisons
Anthonys Nose
Peekskill
Caldwells
Verplancks Pt.
Stoney Pt.
Haverstraw or Warren
Croton R.
Rockland L.
Sing Sing
Nyack
Greensburg or Tarry T.
Erie R.R.
Piermont
Tappan
Dobbs Ferry
Palisades
Yonkers
Kings Br.
Fort Lee
Harlem
Bulls Ferry
Hoboken
Jersey City
New York

Troy
Bath
Albany
Greenbush
Hudson River R.R.
Overslaugh
Castleton
Coeymans
New Baltimore
Schodack
Kinderhook Landing
Coxackie Landing
Stuyvesant
Stockport V.
4 Mile Point Hd. of Ship Navigation
Athens
Hudson
Catskill
Oakhill
German T.
Malden
Tivoli
Saugerties
Glasgow
Barry T.
Lower Redhook
Kingston
Rondout Landing
Rhinebeck Landing
Staatsburg
Pelham
Hyde Park

THE HUDSON RIVER.

Notwithstanding all that has been said and sung, all that has been engraved and painted, and al that has been carved and sculptured in praise of the marvellous beauties of the Rhine,the Rhone, the Po and the Guadalquiver, of Europe, and of the fabled rivers of the voluptuous East, we doubt if any of them can excel the noble Hudson in splendour of scenery variety of embellishment, and that happy blending of simplicity with grandeur, which s clearly characterizes the beautiful "River of the North." To enjoy fully the delightful iews "always changing, always new," which, like golden fringes, adorn this unsurpasse stream from its source to its very mouth, one should take passage on a day boat, when the weather is clear, and the temperature such as to enable him to keep his position on th promenade deck without being chilled by the cold, or suffocated by the heat—although i the hottest weather the part of the boat alluded to is the most comfortable that can be foud. In short, to truly enjoy the beauties of Hudson River scenery, one must have nothig else to do, and if that be well done, there will be neither time nor inclination to do ay thing else. During the summer season several fine boats, equal in size and excellence tany passenger boats in the world, are continually plying upon this river between New 'ork, Albany and Troy, and intermediate points. Some of them start from New York at six, P. M., and arrive at Albany or Troy by daylight next morning. Others, leaving New 'ork at six or seven in the morning, reach the end of the voyage early in the afternoon. Those who consider "time" as the most valuable of earthly things, will take night boa, and, sleeping during the passage, will have passed a thousand beautiful sights, without aving witnessed one of them—but they will have lost no *time*. Others, who consider ti to be like *money*—worth nothing unless it can be expended—will take a day boat, and ese latter worthies we will beg leave to accompany, if they will allow us that privilege Before we start, we will refer our readers to our engraving of the interior of one of t first-class boats, the "Isaac Newton," which, by the way, is a "night boat." The passa on a first-class night boat is usually $1 50 or $2, (6*s*. or 8*s*. sterling,) berths and meals ra at 50 cents each. In times of competition, berths are included in the fare, and somet es the latter is reduced to $1. In the day boats the fare is usually from $1 to $2, mea extra at 50 cents each. Second-class boats often take passengers at half these rates, but they generally take large freights of goods to different points on the river, they mak long stoppages, and the voyage to the tourist becomes tiresome. Distance, from New rk to Albany, 145 miles; to Troy, 150 miles.

The first thing to b done, on entering the boat, is to see that your baggage is properly bestowed, else you wi fancy—if you be at all nervous—that at every stopping-place you see your trunk or pet bag going ashore in some other man's possession—by mistake, of course. This cause you needless anxiety, and subject you to many useless passages up and down t stairway. As some of the river steamers are not so strict or methodical in their mana ment of baggage matters, as the railways are, you can, if they refuse to check your bag e, take the matter into your own hands, and, by searching for the boat's barber—who is obably hunting for *you*, or for any body else from whom he can earn a shilling—you can your baggage safely deposited in his tonsorial sanctum, where it will be safe until the e of the voyage, when you need not trouble yourself at all about *him*, as he will be sur search *you* out, spurred on by the expectation of receiving a shilling (6*d*. sterling) for trouble, which you will cheerfully bestow on one whose watchful care has saved you eal of trouble and anxiety. Your next step is to go to the "ticket office" and purch your ticket for the trip, and make inquiries as to the exact hours for meals, which, ing done, set your watch by the boat's clock, go down below and find out the locality the dining saloon, and the best means of access from the deck; then take a shawl, or ove at—no matter how warm the weather is—it may change

STATE-ROOM SALOON OF THE "ISAAC EWTON."

(HUDSON RIVER STEAMBOAT.)

The River Hudson has been named after its discoverer, Henry Hudson—an Englishman, then in the service of the Dutch—and who, in an exploring expedition, about 250 years ago, was the first to discover this magnificent river, and ascended it as far as the village of Verplanck's Point—in his ship called the "Half Moon." The Indian name of the Hudson was the Shatemuck, in later times it has been termed the River of Mountains, the at River, the North River, and the Rhine of merica.

In the year 7, Robert Fulton, who constructed the fir steamboat in America—if not in the world—rted the steamer "Clermont" on the waters the Hudson—from New York to Albany. engine which worked the Clermont, was bght from England for the purpose.

in an hour—and make your way to the promenade deck, pick out your seat on that side of the boat which you think will keep you *shady*, sit down and make yourself comfortable.

As soon as the boat swings off, you take a parting view of the Battery, and turn your attention to the multitude of vessels of every size and from every clime, moving in every direction, and among which your steamer seems to swim with a celerity and grace of motion, that satisfies you at once that were the river as full again of craft there would be no danger of collision.

Hoboken, N. J., is the first point worthy of notice after leaving the pier. It is one of the lungs of New York, to which the citizens repair in immense numbers on Sundays and fair week days, for the purpose of breathing a little fresh air, drinking a draught of pure water from the Sybil Cave, and taking a walk through the pleasant Elysian Fields, and, perchance, from there to Weehawken, or Bergen Heights.

Passing on we amuse ourselves with watching the movements on the river, and the panoramic view of the city as it passes on in its endless variety of palaces and huts, of riches and poverty, until we arrive at

Bull's Ferry, six miles from the city. This is a favourite summer resort, and many New York merchants and capitalists have beautiful residences here. During the warm season ferry boats are continually plying between this place and the city, the fare being usually 12½ cents per passenger. One mile further on, and we come to

Manhattanville, which may be called the suburban portion of the city. It is a beautiful place, embosomed in the midst of woods and hills, and wears the most charming rural appearance imaginable. Just above the village is Clermont, once the residence of Joseph Bonaparte; and here, also, is the resting-place of Audubon, the great naturalist. Just on the edge of the village is situated the Lunatic Asylum, commanding a high and healthy position, surrounded by forty acres of land, divided into gardens and pleasure grounds. We next come to

Fort Lee.—Just above this place commences the far-famed Palisades, which are composed of bold, precipitous rocks, rising to the height of between five and six hundred feet, and extending along a distance of more than twenty miles. In some respects these grand and imposing precipices resemble the Giant's Causeway in Ireland. Being fringed with brushwood on the top, and dotted here and there at their base with neat little cottages built at the very water's edge, they afford a very fine appearance as the steamer glides swiftly by. The two views we give of the Palisades, one being from the steamer, and the other from the railroad, will convey an idea of their general appearance.

Fort Washington lies nearly opposite Fort Lee, and its history reminds us of the dark and desperate days of the Revolution. In 1776 it fell into the hands of the British, and its garrison of three thousand men were made prisoners of war, but at a cost to the victors of twelve hundred men, and the loss of the ship Mercury, which was so riddled with balls that she sunk soon after the battle. A little further on is Spuyten Devil (spite the devil) Creek, famous in song and story.

Yonkers is one of the most ancient settlements in the neighbourhood of the city. Long before the Revolution it was the home of the famous Phillips's family, of which was Mary Phillips, said to have been the first love of Washington. During the Revolution, Yonkers was the scene of many a conflict between the British and Americans. In 1777 a naval action occurred on the river at this point between the American gunboats and two British frigates. Among the many striking residences to be seen in this place, we may mention Fonthill, built, and once occupied by, Edwin Forrest, the distinguished tragedian. Passing on three miles, we come to

Hastings, a pleasant, thriving village; and two miles beyond, we reach

Dobb's Ferry, named after an old settler who established the first ferry across the river at this point. This also has many scenes connected with the Revolution, not the least interesting of which is the sad story of Arnold and André. Four miles above here is

ALBANY STEAMER PASSING THE PALISADES,
ON HER WAY TO NEW YORK.

VIEW OF THE PALISADES FROM YONKERS STATION.

SUNNYSIDE, IRVINGTON.

Irvington, named after the distinguished author, Washington Irving, whose beautiful cottage of *Sunnyside*—a representation of which we present——although lying close to the river, is so completely smothered in dense shrubbery, that it is hardly discernible from the decks of the passing steamers. A little further up, and on the opposite side of the river, we come to

Piermont, which was formerly the eastern terminus of the Erie Railroad. The river is here three miles in breadth, and the shores are so bold and picturesque as to present to the beholder from the river, some of the most striking and attractive pictures to be seen on the route. Two or three miles back of Piermont is the old town of Tappan, where Washington for a time held his head-quarters. It was here also that the unfortunate Major André was imprisoned and executed. The jail in which he was confined is still standing, as also is the house in which Washington resided. Pursuing our course, we pass the village of *Nyack*, on the same side of the river, and come to

Tarrytown, which lies on the opposite side. This place is doubly famous. In the Revolution it was the scene of many a rough and sanguinary encounter between the lawless bands of the British and American armies, known as Skinners and Cow-boys, who chose the ground hereabouts, as being between the two encampments, as the scene for continual strife. Here, too, in the very centre of the town, is the spot where Major André was arrested by the patriots Paulding, Williams and Van Wart, just as he was returning to the British encampment, after his interview with the

PAULDING, WILLIAMS AND VAN WART'S MONUMENT.

traitorous Arnold. We present a faithful view of the monument which has been erected to commemorate that great event. Tarrytown is also famous in the history of old Diedrich Knickerbocker, immortalized by Washington Irving. About two miles up the valley, at the back of the village, is the place known as "Sleepy Hollow," so graphically described by Washington Irving in his interesting legend. By turning to our description of the Catskill Mountains, a correct sketch of one of the many views to be had at "Sleepy Hollow" will be found. Leaving Tarrytown, we sail on for about five miles, and then touch at

Sing Sing.—This village is built upon a hill slope, which rises to a height of 200 feet, and presents a fine appearance from the river. The principal object of curiosity here is the *State Prison,* which is a massive structure, the main building being 484 feet long, 44 feet wide, and five stories high. The area covered by the whole establishment is 130 acres. The prison contains one thousand single cells, which unfortunately are almost always filled. Two miles above the village the Croton River, from which the City of New York receives its supply of water, enters the Hudson. We give a view of the Croton Dam on next page.

Opposite Sing Sing is a commanding height 250 feet above the river, upon the top of which is Rockland Lake, a sketch of which during winter we present. Three miles onward we pass the village of

Haverstraw, and three miles beyond that we come to

Stony Point. This is another of the famous places which are embalmed in American Revolutionary history. Between this place and Verplanck's point, which lies opposite, was established what was called the *King's Ferry,* which was commanded by forts on both shores. In May, 1779, these were taken by the British, but, on the following July, Stony Point was retaken by the Americans, and the works destroyed. A light-house now stands upon the extremity of Stony Point.

Verplanck's Point is celebrated as being the place at which Henry Hudson anchored his good ship, the "Half Moon," on his first voyage up the Hudson River. The surprise of the Indians in those days may be imagined, at seeing for the first time, a vessel of such proportions invading their quiet waters. A writer records the following incident as having occurred at that time:—

"Filled with wonder, the Indians came flocking to the ship in boats, but their curiosity ended in a tragedy. One of them, overcome by acquisitiveness, crawled up the rudder, entered the cabin window, and stole a pillow and a few articles of wearing apparel. The ship's boats were sent for the stolen articles, and when one of the natives, who had leaped into the water, caught hold of the side of the shallop, his hand was cut off by the stroke of a sword, and he was drowned. This was the first blood shed by these voyagers. Intelligence of it spread over the country, and the Indians hated the white man ever after."

Leaving *Verplanck's Point,* the river narrows considerably, and the voyager's eye is attracted to the

Highlands of the Hudson, which begin to rise at this point. On the east shore is the pretty village of Peekskill, and on the west is seen the rugged front of Dunderberg, or Thunder Mountain, at whose base the little village and landing of Caldwell are nestled. It was at this little place that such active measures were taken a few years ago in searching for the sunken treasures of Captain Kyd, who was supposed to have scuttled one of his rich ships in this neighbourhood. After a laborious search of many months, with diving-bells and other submarine apparatus, the adventurers gave up their profitless speculation, receiving only the jeers and ridicule of the people as their reward, instead of the weighty bullion which they had anticipated.

As the steamer proceeds up the river, the tourist, if he has ever sailed up Loch Lomond (Scotland), will be forcibly struck with the similarity in appearance which the Hudson here presents to it. At one time you will be sailing past islands possessed of all the beauty of Ellen's Isle on Loch Katrine (Scot.), with high hills wooded to their tops on each side, whilst, proceeding onwards, the channel of the river appears completely blocked up, till the steamer takes a turn round the base of one of the hills, only to open up another scene of

The above sketch represents a view of the Croton Dam, from whence issues the water supplied to New York City. This Dam is 250 feet long, 40 feet high, 70 feet wide at the bottom, and 7 feet at the top. From it the water proceeds through tunnels in the soha rocks, crossing valleys by embankments, and rivers by bridges until it reaches the Harlem River, across which it is carried through iron pipes laid on the roadway of the magnificent High Bridge, of which we give a sketch elsewhere. The building and other necessary equipments connected with bringing the water into New York, occupied between 7 and 8 years, and cost about 14 millions of dollars. The fountain reservoir is about 40 miles from New York. Croton Station, on the Hudson River Railroad, is the nearest station to it, and, independent of the fine situation and scenery about the vicinity of the dam, the spot may be seen at Pine's Bridge, (seen in the foreground of the above sketch,) where Major André crossed the Croton River after his interview with Arnold.

ICE CUTTING AT ROCKLAND LAKE, NEAR NEW YORK.

Rockland Lake, a clear and crystal body of water, about four miles in circumference. It is from this beautiful lake that the citizens of New York obtain their supply of ice during the summer months, and if *use* be the criterion of *worth*, no mine in California has given more wealth to the world than has been cut from the frozen bosom of Rockland Lake.

In the above engraving will be seen the Ice Company's men busy at work reaping the icy harvest, and storing it in the ice-house at the edge of the lake. That ice-house is capable of stowing away about 20,000 tons of ice, and preserving it completely from the effects of the external heat during the summer season.

great magnificence, and to reveal the Highland beauties of hill and dale, clothed in their brightest summer foliage. The Highlands—as they are well named—extend along the course of the river about 25 miles, and during the whole trip, no portion will be better enjoyed until the last height is reached near Newburg. On rounding Dunderberg Mountain, will be seen

Anthony's Nose, 1128 feet high, which is as high as any respectable nose can be expected to *turn up*. Two miles further on, the *Sugar Loaf* reaches up to an elevation of 806 feet—whilst on the west side *Buttermilk Falls* are seen descending over the face of the hill. In some of these Highland passes on the river, are sometimes to be found numbers of wind-bound vessels, tacking about, and presenting a beautiful sight as they wriggle themselves like so many eels, in their attempts to get into a broader part of the river. Before reaching the next stopping-place we have to round

Constitution Island, which, in Revolutionary times, was fortified, the remains of the works still being perceptible. From this island to West Point a chain was thrown across the river as an obstruction to the enemy's ships. Some links of this defence are still to be seen in the neighbourhood. We now reach

West Point. The Revolutionary reminiscences connected with this place, the unrivalled beauty of the scenery, and its being the seat of the principal military school in the country, all combine to make this one of the most attractive points on the river. It is for this reason that we have devoted so much space to pictorial illustrations of West Point and vicinity, and these we shall distribute through our pages, without much regard to their immediate connection with our descriptive matter.

The United States Military Academy at West Point, was established by Congress in 1802, and is entirely controlled and supported by government. There are a large number of cadets here, who are educated gratuitously in a course of studies through a period of five years, and embracing every theme required for a thorough knowledge of the military art. At the expiration of his studies, each student is expected to continue eight years in the public service unless sooner excused.

In the time of the Revolution West Point was considered a place of great importance, as it was the great key to the river, and it was this place that the infamous Arnold would have given into the hands of the British, had not André, the agent in the affair of treachery, been so providentially arrested at Tarrytown, as before stated. If the tourist has time, he will be well repaid by spending at least one day in a visit to West Point, and in examining its many points of interest. On leaving West Point, we proceed on until we come to

Cronest, which towers to a height of 1428 feet, and is called one of the grandest mountains in the Highland range. George P. Morris thus sings of this prominent peak:

> "Where the Hudson's wave, o'er silvery sands,
>   Winds through the hills afar,
> And Cronest, like a monarch stands,
>   Crowned with a single star."

After passing this romantic locality, we reach *Butter Hill*, or, as Mr. N. P. Willis has re-christened it, the *Storm King*, which is 1500 feet high, and the last high range of hills on that side of the river. Passing on, we reach *Cold Spring*, which is built upon a steep ascent, from behind which rises *Bull Hill*, whose shadow falls upon *Undercliff*, the rural residence of George P. Morris, the poet. A short distance further on, and we come to

Cornwall Landing, above which is the seat of Mr. N. P. Willis, named *Idlewild*, surrounded with all the natural romantic beauties which we fancy any poet would delight to dwell amongst. Shortly after leaving this beautiful place, we come to the important town of *Newburg*. (See page 18&21.)

KOSCIUSCO'S MONUMENT, WEST POINT.

Thaddeus Kosciusco was born in Lithuania, in 1756, and was educated in Warsaw, Poland. He afterwards removed to Paris, where he continued his studies. While in this latter city he made the acquaintance of Dr. Franklin, who, on learning the intention of the young adventurer to visit America for the purpose of aiding in the struggle for independence, gave him a flattering letter of introduction to General Washington. On his arrival in America, he was appointed engineer in the army, with the rank of colonel, in October, 1776, and soon after went to West Point and superintended the erection of the defences of that place. He was highly esteemed by the army, and received the thanks of Congress for his services. At the close of the war he returned to Warsaw, where he remained until the war of

VIEW FROM FORT PUTNAM, WEST POINT.

VIEW DOWN THE HUDSON, AT WEST POINT.

1794, when he was appointed generalissimo of the Polish army, with the power of dictation. Being taken prisoner, he was sent to St. Petersburg, where he was kept in confinement until the death of the Empress Catherine. In 1797, the gallant Pole again visited America, and was rewarded by Congress with an especial grant. He afterwards retired to Switzerland, where he lived in peaceful seclusion until his death in 1817. The above monument was erected by the cadets of West Point, as a tribute of respect for his many private virtues and acknowledged worth.

The above engraving will serve as a companion picture to the one given below. This one shows us the river on its downward course, and takes in both shores, as seen from the water. Although these views are photographed from

VIEW FROM THE BATTERY, WEST POINT.

Nature, and give as faithful an outline of living scenes as it is possible to present, yet it must be confessed that no art, however high may be its attainment, can do exact justice to the exquisite subjects we have endeavoured to illustrate. To thoroughly enjoy these splendid views, one must look with his own eyes, and hear with his own ears, for in scenes like the above the very murmurings of the atmosphere "bear pleasant sounds along."

The view given of the Hudson River, as seen from the Battery at West Point, is as pleasing to the eye as it is truthful to nature. The opposite range of mountains stretching into the distance as far as the eye can reach; while the majestic river winds its way in graceful curves, bearing upon its placid bosom the buoyant steamer, which cleaves its unerring course as true, and almost as swift as the arrow speeds from the bow, leaving the smaller craft to wage a harmless warfare against their, sometimes, natural enemies—wind and tide; —all these, and a host of other indescribable scenes, serve to make a picture that is seldom equalled even in this region of magnificent sights.

The other engraving of West Point was taken from Fort Putnam. This fort was erected in the days of the Revolution in consequence of its commanding position, it being situated on the top of a hill nearly 600 feet above the river's edge. Its elevated position, from which not only the river, but the country for miles around is plainly visible, makes it an admirable point from which to photograph the scenic beauties which are so lavishly spread around this highly-favoured region.

DADE'S MONUMENT, WEST POINT.

Newburg, with its 12,000 inhabitants, finely situated on the face of the hill. To the south of the town is the spot which once formed the head-quarters of Washington, a representation of which we give on another page. (p. 21.)

LABORATORY AND HOTEL AT WEST POINT.

The "Laboratory" building, represented in our engraving, is connected with the United States Military Academy at West Point. The "Hotel" is built upon the brow of the hill, and is approached by a good carriage road from the landing; or the pedestrian may reach it by a foot-path, much shorter, but more difficult. The view from the observatory of the hotel is very fine and far-reaching. The windings of the beautiful river, the towns and villages that fringe its banks on either side, the broad expanse of country, spreading in every direction, and chequered with innumerable fields, gardens, orchards, and strips of woodland hemmed in by the dim range of far-distant mountains,—all these, and many more enchanting lights and shades of busy life greet the eye of the beholder, and fills the heart with emotions indescribably pleasing.

Here is another fine view taken from West Point, and looking across the river. The high ground, from which this picture was taken, is a favourite place of resort in the summer time for the citizens of West Point, as well as for such strangers as find more pleasure in viewing dame Nature out of doors than in mixing with steaming, fuming, fretting human nature within doors. On a pleasant, moonlight eve, one could hardly select a finer spot than this, whether to whisper love into the ear of the chosen one, to hold a social converse with an esteemed friend, or to sit or walk alone, and "inly ruminate."

ACROSS THE HUDSON AT WEST POINT.

WASHINGTON'S LANDING-PLACE.

This beautifully romantic spot, represented in the accompanying engraving, is situated on Denny's Point, just opposite Newburg. When Washington held his head-quarters in the old stone mansion, a short distance south of Newburg village, he was in the habit of frequently crossing the river, for the purpose of spending an hour or two at this point, which subsequently took his name. Here the great chief would sit and contemplate the quiet beauties of the scene spread out before him. And here, it is, perhaps, not too much to suppose, he entered into some of those calm but serious reflections resulting in the formation of those great plans which soon after obtained victory over the British army, in the unconditional surrender of the claims of England, and in the complete recognition of the independence of the United Colonies.

The following engraving represents one of the many beautiful villas which adorn the banks of the Hudson. These residences are mostly owned and occupied by retired merchants and other men of wealth from New York, who, tired with the noise and confusion of the great city, come here to eke out their remaining days in the quiet and wholesome enjoyments of rural life. These villas are generally erected on or near the summits of gentle slopes of ground facing the river, and just far enough away from the noisy town to be free from annoyance by its bustle and excitement, and just near enough to have quick and easy access to its markets and stores. There are some fine villas on the Hudson, which are only occupied during the summer months, their owners preferring the gaieties of the city to the sober quiet of the country, during the long winter season.

MR. SARGENT'S VILLA, NEAR PEEKSKILL.

WASHINGTON'S HEAD-QUARTERS NEWBURGH.

The house which Washington occupied is still standing, and is an object of much pride with the citizens. It was here that the Revolutionary army was finally disbanded at the close of the war in 1783. Opposite Newburg, on the east side of the river, is *Break Neck Mountain*, which was supposed to have resembled a *Turk's face*, and can be easily seen from the deck of the steamer when approaching Pallopel's Island. The story connected with this mountain is as follows:

"Some Irishmen were quarrying for granite once, when one of them put a blast of powder before the Turk's face, saying he thought the old fellow would like to have his nose blowed, and the nose was completely blowed away. The admirers of the curious and beautiful think that the Irishman, who was shortly after killed, was justly hurried from the world for his barbarity to the works of Nature."

A view of the defaced *face* as it appears now is presented on a following page.

Fishkill, which lies nearly opposite Newburg, numbers about 2,000 inhabitants, and contains many fine residences of retired New York merchants. Besides the Revolutionary legends connected with the history of Fishkill, it possesses an interest as being the scene of many of the leading incidents in Cooper's novel of the "Spy." Two miles northeast of Fishkill Landing is the Verplanck House, interesting as having once been the head-quarters of Baron Steuben, and the place in which the famous *Society of the Cincinnati* was organized in 1783.

Passing *Low Point*, three miles above Fishkill, and the villages of *New Hamburg*, *Marlborough* and *Barnegat*, we reach the largest city on the river between New York and Albany,

Poughkeepsie, which is 75 miles from New York, and the half-way station on the Hudson River Railroad. It is a fine city, containing 15,000 inhabitants, and is a place of much business importance. It was settled by the Dutch 150 years ago, but at present bears but little evidence of its Teutonic origin. It is built upon an elevated plane, half a mile east of the river, and is regularly and symmetrically laid out. Professor Morse, the inventor of the magnetic telegraph, and B. J. Lossing, the historian, reside here.

New Paltz Landing is just opposite Poughkeepsie, and is the landing-place for passengers from the town of New Paltz, which lies eight miles west. There is a ferry from here to Poughkeepsie.

Hyde Park and *Placentia* are five miles beyond, situated on the east side of the river. Placentia is the residence of the veteran author, James K. Paulding, who is passing a green and healthful old age between his books and the fields, and has chosen a spot from which some of the finest views on the river are presented. Passing Staatsburg, a small stopping-place on the railroad, we come to Rondout.

SCENE ON RONDOUT CREEK, STATE OF NEW YORK.

The above view represents a scene on the small stream of the Rondout, which takes its rise in Sullivan county, N. Y., about 100 miles from New York, and enters the Hudson at Eddyville, near Rondout, 90 miles from New York. The Delaware and Hudson Canal follows the stream all the way through the valley in which the Rondout flows.

Rondout, a village on the Hudson, takes its name from the creek, and is the stepping-place for the steamers between New York and Albany, for Kingston, three miles distant, the most important town between these two cities.

The view given above was engraved from a photograph by D. Huntingdon, and portrays a scene of great beauty.

A writer on this scene says:—"In it we have the constituents of many pictures which reproduce our characteristic land-features, viz.: repose, grace, richness of foliage, softness of sky, gentle flow of water—all harmonizing to produce a very inspiriting sensation in the mind."

VIEW OF THE TURK'S FACE, ON THE HUDSON.

Rondout, which is situated on Rondout Creek, (a view of which is on last page,) is the terminus of the Delaware and Hudson Canal, through which large supplies of coal are brought into market.

Kingston, a thriving and pleasant town of 6,000 inhabitants, is situated on an elevated plain three miles back of Rondout. It was settled by the Dutch near two hundred years ago, and in 1777 was burned by the British. The first constitution of the State of New York was framed and adopted in a house still standing.

Rhinebeck is on the railway, opposite Rondout, to which it is connected by a ferry. We now pass in rapid succession the towns of Saugerties and Malden, on the west, and Tivoli and Germantown, on the east side of the river, and during our voyage our eyes are attracted by the new and magnificent features which present themselves before us. To the east, the pleasant villages and graceful scenery along the banks of the river appear in striking contrast to the wild, bold ranges of the Shawangunk and Catskill Mountains, which loom up in the west, and form fresh and charming pictures at every step of our progress. *Oakhill* is a station on the railway for the opposite town of

Catskill, which lies on the west side of the river. Those who intend visiting the *Catskill Mountains* must debark here, where they will find carriages to take them to any part desired. A full description of these mountains will be found in another part of this book. The town of Catskill of itself presents many objects of attraction. Rising with a gradual slope from the margin of the creek to a high elevation towards the north, its pretty cottages and elegant villas are seen to the best advantage from the river in front, as well as from the mountains which rise on the west of the town. As the steamer passes the mouth of the creek, an excellent distant view of the Catskill Mountains is obtained, with the Mountain House standing like a speck on the top of a ridge. The distance to the Mountain House from the creek is about ten miles.

Hudson.—This beautiful city lies on the opposite shore from Catskill, and about 5 miles further up the river. Commercially and topographically this is one of the most important towns on the Hudson. The main street commences at the river—from a bold promontory, called Promenade Hill, which rises abruptly full 60 feet above the water—and running through the centre of the city, terminates at the foot of Prospect Hill, which rises to an altitude of 200 feet, and from whose top some of the finest views imaginable are to be seen. The populous city, spread out like a map, just below; the noble Hudson stretching its tortuous length for miles on either side; and the lofty heights of Catskill looming up like great clouds in the distance, can all be taken in at a glance.

From Hudson a trip can be made to Columbia, 5 miles distant, and to Claverack Falls, 8 miles off. Lebanon Springs, 36 miles from Hudson, are reached by taking the Hudson & Berkshire line of cars.

Shaker Village, is at New Lebanon, and about 6 miles from the Springs. If the tourist can devote time enough for a brief visit to the interesting village of the Society of Shakers, he will observe a place of primitive and simple life that will amply repay him for all the trouble and expense he may incur.

Our voyage is now drawing to a close. The route begins to lose much of its Highland character, but is still of a highly picturesque and interesting description. Directly opposite Hudson is Athens, a pretty village of 1500 inhabitants. Passing on we successively reach Stockport, Coxsackie and Stuyvesant, which are thriving little towns of from 1,000 to 2,000 inhabitants each, and come to *Kinderhook Landing*, five miles back of which lies the town of

Kinderhook. This place is somewhat famous as having been the birth-place of Martin Van Buren, ex-President of the United States, who still resides here on, his estate of "Lindenwold," some two miles south of the village.

New Baltimore and *Coeymans* are now passed on the left, and *Schodac* and *Castleton* on the right, and a further sail of 8 miles brings us to the end of our present journey, and our boat draws up gracefully to her pier in Albany, a brief description of which we will append to this route.

ALBANY.

Albany is the Capital of the Empire State, and at the present time contains a population of about 65,000. The place was founded by the Dutch, in 1614, and was the second European settlement made in the original thirteen States—Jamestown (Virginia), having been the first.

It was called successively Fort Orange, Beaver Wyck, and Williamstadt, before it received its present name, which was conferred by the English—when they took possession, in 1664—in honor of James, Duke of York and Albany, afterwards James the Second. Albany is advantageously situated for commerce, at the head of sloop navigation on the Hudson, and having communication by means of canals with Lakes Erie, Ontario and Champlain, and by railway with New York, Boston, Buffalo and other less prominent places.

The principal object of attraction is the State House, which is an imposing edifice, standing on the top of Capitol Hill. It is 115 feet long, and 90 feet wide. The walls are 50 feet high, and crowned by a dome, on which stands a statue of Justice, 11 feet high, with the usual sword in the right hand, and balance in the left. Near by are situate the State Hall, a beautiful marble building, containing the various offices of the State Government; and the City Hall, also of marble, and topped by a gilded dome.

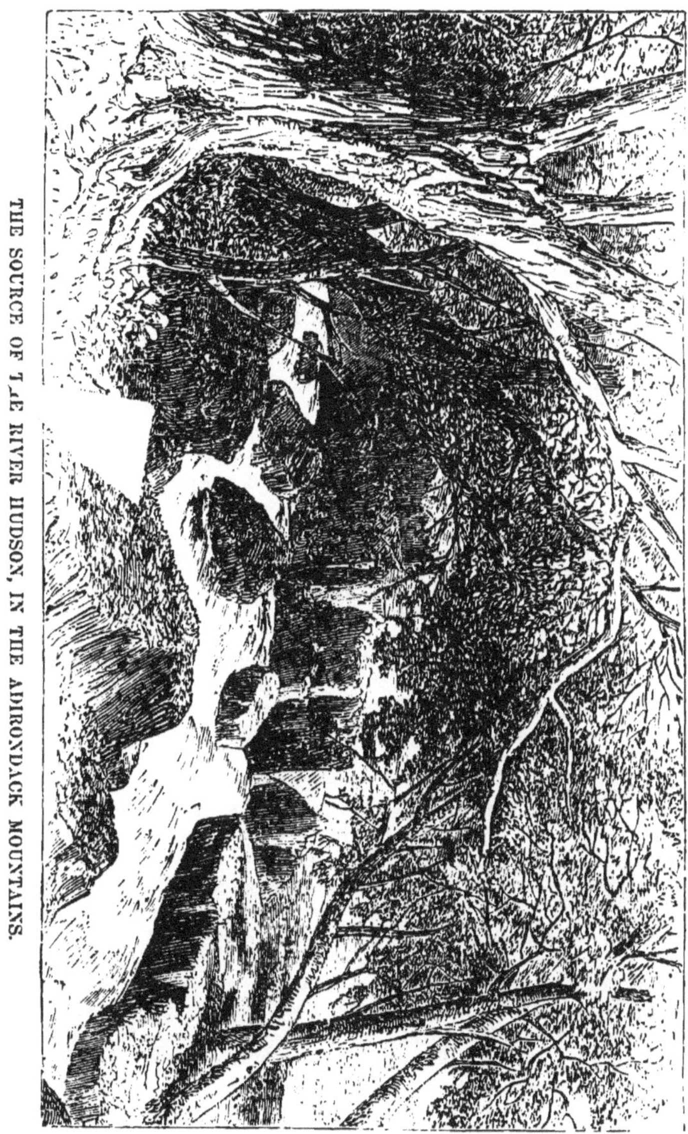

THE SOURCE OF THE RIVER HUDSON, IN THE ADIRONDACK MOUNTAINS.

The view here presented is a scene in the Adirondack mountains, in the vicinity of, and west of Lake Champlain. Some of the peaks of these mountains (Mount Marcy) rise as high as 5464 feet above the level of tide water in the River Hudson. Up in that mountainous region does that noble river take its rise. From there it proceeds almost due south, for about 300 miles, until it enters the Atlantic, through the harbour of New York. The Adirondacks are famous as a deer-hunting country.

Albany is distinguished for her educational and literary institutions: among the most celebrated being the Albany Academy, erected at a cost of $100,000; the Dudley Observatory, the Medical College, and the State Normal School. The State Library—open to the public—has 27,000 volumes of choice books; the Young Men's Association 8,000 volumes, and the Apprentices' Library 3,000 volumes. The city contains over 40 church-edifices.

Albany, as seen from the river, presents an effective appearance—the ground rising gradually from the shore to an elevation of 225 feet in the range of a mile westward. State street, the widest thoroughfare in the city, ascends in a straight line from the water, to the height crowned by the State Capitol. The distance from Albany to Buffalo is 298 miles; to Boston, 200 miles; and to New York, 145 miles.

SHAKER COMMUNITY.

"Shaker seeds and herbs," and "Shaker flannels," are amongst the multifarious signs exhibited at doors, and in the windows of retail stores throughout the United States—the excellence of these articles, as sold by a section of the Society of Friends in America—generally known as "The Shakers"—having rendered them famous throughout the country. The stranger in America who is desirous of seeing something of one of the "Institutions" peculiar to this country, may easily visit one of the Shaker villages when at New York, by taking the railroad, or steamboat up the Hudson, to Hudson City, 118 miles from New York, and thence for a few miles per rail to Lebanon Springs, in the County of Columbia, State of New York. In this trip, the tourist can enjoy the trip up the Hudson—visit Lebanon Springs, and the Quaker Settlement, two miles from there—the Catskill Mountains, in the vicinity—noticed elsewhere—and all in the course of a few days, at comparatively little expense.

The Society whose establishment we at present purpose noticing, reside at the Shaker village of New Lebanon, as we have said, two miles from Lebanon Springs, in a beautiful and fertile agricultural district. The village is situated on the face of a hill, and commands a fine view of the valley in the vicinity and surrounding country.

The village is exclusively tenanted by the members of the Community. The principal building consists of a large Meeting-House, where the devotional exercises are conducted, and in the summer time, on Sundays, in the presence of vast numbers of strangers who are sojourning at the Springs. The Extract House is another of the chief buildings. In it is the Laboratory, where the herbs, and tinctures from them, are pressed by means of crushing mills, vacuum pan, etc., under a skillful chemist, one of themselves. The estimation in which such are held, may be judged of from the fact, that in one year about 14,000 pounds' weight have been sold—the extracts of butternut and dandelion forming two of the principal ones sold. In another part of the village is the Seed House, formerly the old Meeting-House, near which is the Tannery, Dairy, and workshops where wooden-ware, door-mats, etc., are made. The Herb House, with its drying rooms, store rooms, etc., is another portion of the manufacturing premises. There, about 70 tons of herbs and roots—the produce of about 75 acres of their garden land—are pressed annually, by means of a hydraulic press of 300 tons pressure. In various parts of the building may be seen both men, women, and children busily engaged in the different processes of manufacturing the articles named, or packing them up ready for market.

The Community at New Lebanon consist of about 500 persons, divided into eight families, as they are called, each family being presided over by two elders and two elderesses, each of whom have an equal position in the management, and to whose orders the members yield perfect obedience.

The management of the temporal affairs of the Society is entrusted to trustees, who are elected by the ministry and elders, and who are legally in possession of all real estate belonging to the community. The chief business trustee is a Mr. Edward Fowler, a man of about 65 years of age.

The principles they profess are Christian, although their views of Christianity are peculiar. It would take up too much of our space to go into detail respecting these; but we may briefly say that they believe the millennium has come; that theirs is the millennial Church; that marriage prevents people from being assimilated to the character of Christ; that the wicked are punished only for a season; that the judgment-day has begun in their Church being established; and that their state of existence is the beginning of heaven. They entertain the doctrines of the spiritualists to a certain extent, and profess to have had their regular "manifestations of the spirit" for many years past, and that, for instance, the hymns they sing—both words and music—are revealed to them every week in time for devotional exercises on Sunday.

In the Meeting-House they assemble at about half past 10 o'clock every Sunday morning, and, Quaker-like, the sexes are seated separately, with the men and women facing each other; all the men, excepting the elders, being in their shirt sleeves, and wearing blue cotton and woolen trowsers and vests, with calf-skin shoes, gray stockings, and large turned-down collars, as seen in figure 1 in engraving of costume. The women wear, for the most part, pure white cotton dresses, with white cotton handkerchiefs spread over their necks and shoulders, with a white lawn square tied over their heads, with boots similar in appearance to the high-heeled boots lately in fashion—the fashion of the time when the Society was established—and made of a light blue prunella. See figure 7 in engraving of costume.

SHAKER COSTUME.

The above engraving represents the various costumes worn by the Shakers, both at home, and when from home. Figures 1 and 7 represent the worship costume, and attitude of man and woman. Figure 2, that of a field-labourer, or storekeeper's assistant. Figure 3, an elder. Figures 4 and 5, travelling costume, and Figure 6, a half-dress costume.

After sitting a short time in silence, the members from the extreme ends of the room approach the centre, when the seats are removed, and the whole congregation place themselves in marching order in serried rows, three or four men and women alternately. Whilst thus standing silently—the women with their eyes looking to the floor—one of the elders in the midst of them makes a few remarks, after which a hymn is sung to a very lively tune, the whole of the congregation keeping time with their feet

After the hymn the worshippers commence a dance, an illustration of one of the movements or steps of which we give. The dance consists of a series of evolutions of different forms, presenting in each all the precision of well-trained pupils, moving as if with only one step. The illustration will give an idea of a backward and forward dance or march, with

SHAKERS' RELIGIOUS DANCE.

them keeping time to the hymns they sing, at the same time, following the example, as they say, of David, when he danced before the Lord with all his might. After this, and when all the seats are replaced, and the congregation seated as before, one of the elders delivers a discourse, when the seats are removed again to give place to another dance of a different style, and to another hymn. This time the dance is of a more lively character, with the action of the arms, thrown up and down, and clapping of hands in regular order. In this way are several hymns sung and danced to, and addresses delivered; and however much parties, on reading the accounts of such, may be disposed to smile, no one can witness the devotional exercises of these people, such as they are, without being impressed with feelings of the deepest respect and solemnity; and however much they may differ from the Shakers in opinion, they will be ready to give them full credit for thorough conscientiousness, and faith in what they believe to be right.

Occasionally the "spirit manifests itself" by one or more of the congregation getting up and dancing or whirling round and round with extraordinary rapidity, and the parties apparently being perfectly unconscious of every thing passing around them. In this way will they continue to whirl and dance for nearly an hour without intermission.

As may be well known, all property belonging to the Society is held in common by the members. All who join it do so voluntarily, after perusing the rules and regulations of the Society, which are submitted to all before they join. The Society is divided into three divisions, or classes, viz.: the senior, junior, and noviciate class. The senior class dedicate themselves and all they are possessed of "to the service of God and the support of the pure gospel, forever," after they have had time for reflection and experience. After being thus admitted as partners in the Community, the relationship is binding forever. The second class of members are those who have no families, but who, in joining the Society, retain the ownership of any private property they had when they entered it. It is according to the laws that if any one leaves the Community they can take nothing with them but what they brought; that they receive no wages for the services they may have performed, and cannot recover any property they may have presented to the Community. The noviciates, again, are those who, on joining the Society, choose to live by themselves and retain the management of their temporal affairs in their own hands. Such are received as sisters and brothers so long as they fulfil the requirements of the Society in every other respect.

Every one—male and female—works, from the preacher down to the youngest child who is able; and not a moment of the hours of labour is occupied but by the busy and attentive performance of their duties.

Throughout their workshops, meeting-houses, dwellings, etc., the utmost order prevails, accompanied by the most scrupulous cleanliness of place and person. Although they have none of the anxieties of life, or that frightful spectre—the fear of want—ever before them, and with no personal or private ambition to carry out, yet all are willing, diligent, and faithful workers, and all appear to be cheerful, comfortable and happy.

The Community at New Lebanon are, from all we can understand, a most intelligent body. They pursue the same system of education as that of the common schools of the United States, for although they lead a life of celibacy after they join the body, the children of those who come from the "outer world" are regularly taught and brought up in the doctrines and with the ideas of the Community, and from that source, as well as receiving all orphan children who are sent to them, there is a never-failing supply of scholars. The children are dressed similarly to grown-up members. They possess an excellent library, and from the newspapers regularly received, the members are kept "posted up" as to whatever is going on in the wicked world around them.

Their conduct and character, from all accounts, is of the most exemplary kind, living up, in a high degree, to the principles they profess. In their relations with the world around them their business character for honour and uprightness is most undoubted, whilst the articles they manufacture stand deservedly high in public estimation, the very term "Shaker" being a sort of guarantee that the article is genuine.

They carry on their botanical and all other operations in the most scientific manner, and have machinery of the most improved description for enabling them to produce the articles manufactured in the best possible manner.

We may mention the somewhat singular fact, of this society, having taken root so far back as exactly one hundred years ago, in the City of Manchester (Eng.). In the year 1758, a woman named Ann Stanley, then the wife of a blacksmith, embraced the views of Shakerism from the disciples of some French religionists who held these, or similar views there, but suffering great persecution on account of her belief, she, along with a few others, emigrated to America, where she founded a Community at Niskayuna, (Watervliet,) near Albany, where the sect still have a Community. When she arrived in America, she took her maiden name of Lee, and thus the name of Mother Ann Lee is devoutly remembered till this day by the sect, they looking upon her, as, they say, the revelation of the female nature of God to man, in the same way as *The Christ* was manifested in the person of Jesus, as the revelation of the male nature of God to man. During a great revival movement in 1780, large numbers joined Ann Lee's Community, and since then they have spread into different sections of the States—now numbering eighteen Communities—with a total of about 4,000 members, and affording a curious, interesting, and instructive feature in social economies.

SCENE IN THE CATSKILL MOUNTAINS.

One of the most agreeable trips for the tourist, when at New York, is for him to visit the famous scenery of the Catskills. There, a variety of wood, river, and mountain scenery will be enjoyed, not to be met with in most places.

The trip there and back, can be made in 3 or 4 days from New York, and at not much expense.

The charge at the Mountain House is $2.50 (or 10s., stg.,) per day—although cheaper accommodation is to be had as well.

Near the Mountain House is said to be the site where Mr. Washington Irving located the scene of his celebrated novel of "Rip Van Winkle."

Few places of summer resort are more frequented by tourists, whether as artists in search of some charming scenery to study, the invalid in quest of bracing air, or the general traveller in search of the "lions" in America.

JOHN B. DUNHAM,

MANUFACTURER OF THE

OVER STRUNG

GRAND & SQUARE

PIANOFORTES.

Manufactory and Ware Room, 75 to 85 East Thirteenth Street,

NEAR BROADWAY, NEW YORK.

EACH INSTRUMENT IS WARRANTED FOR FIVE YEARS.

PRICES MODERATE.

THE AMERICAN SOLIDIFIED MILK

Prepared near Amenia, in Dutchess Co. N. Y.

Is simply the richest Milk from the best dairies in that well-known county, EVAPORATED at a low temperature, and crystalized upon refined white loaf sugar.

The whole medical profession, as shown by the reports made to various societies, declare it invaluable for infants and invalids. AS IT WILL KEEP FOR YEARS IN ANY CLIMATE, it is indispensable to officers of the army and navy, families traveling by land or sea—but especially for those living at the South, or in hot climates, where Milk is dear or not to be had. It is the only way to procure PURE MILK IN LARGE CITIES, besides being the most economical, for the consumer pays each day only for what is used—not for what sours or is wasted.

For Sale in Packages of various sizes, by the Principal Druggists, Grocers and Ship Chandlers throughout the Union.

For Descriptive Pamphlet and List of Prices, address,

Agency American Solidified Milk Company,

73 LIBERTY STREET, NEW YORK.

A good, general view of these mountains is obtained from the deck of the steamers which pass up and down upon the Hudson.

Strangers take either the Albany steamer, from New York, or Albany, to Catskill, on the Hudson, (111 miles from New York) or the Hudson River Railroad to Oakhill Station, thence per ferry across. From Catskill Village, passengers are conveyed per stage to the Mountain House, 12 miles distant, but the road being very steep, it takes 4 hours to go that distance.

The first view we present, "Scene in the Catskill Mountains," is from a painting by J. F. Kensett, an American artist, the only objection to which we have is, the introduction of two of the aborigines—of the district, we presume—a fault rather common, we think, amongst American artists, to give effect in pictures, whilst such figures can now only be introduced with truth in such districts as Minnesota.

THE UPPER OR SYLVAN LAKE—CATSKILL MOUNTAINS.

The other engravings which follow are without any such additions, being from photographs, taken last year of the scenes represented. To quote from a writer who has visited this locality :—

"The ride to the foot of the mountain is not specially interesting; but the ascent, by a very circuitous route, from every successive opening and turn of which some new and more extensive vista is presented to the eye continually, is in a high degree inspiring and delightful. And when at length the lofty eminence is reached, there opens, from the front of the noble edifice, a prospect of vast extent and beauty; embracing an apparently endless succession of woods and waters, farms and villages, towns and cities, spread out as in a boundless panorama, over which all inequalities of surface are overlooked. The beautiful Hudson appears narrowed in the distance, with numerous vessels scattered along its silvery line, discerned as far as the eye can reach, by their canvas gleaming in the sun, and with the trailing cloud of smoke from steamboats almost constantly in sight.

"The view embraces an area of about 70 miles north and south. Far in the eastern outline rise the Taghanic Mountains, and the highlands of Connecticut and Massachusetts. To the left are seen the Green Mountains of Vermont, stretching away in the north till their blue summits are blended with the sky. At other times all the prospect below is enveloped in a rolling sea of mist and cloud, surging with the wind, and presenting ever new and fanciful forms to the sight. Thunder storms are not unfrequently seen passing below the spectator, while the atmosphere is delightfully clear and cool around him."

The preceding engraving represents one of two lakes of great beauty, which lie close together, overlooked from the north mountain, and a short way from the Mountain House Hotel. All who are acquainted with this beautiful sheet of water, will at once recognize it in the above sketch, which we have had engraved from one of the series of photographs taken there last year. For a pleasant walk alongside its shores, a row on its waters, or for practising the "gentle art" with fishing-rod and line, few spots present greater attractions.

KAUTERSKILL FALLS.

The Sylvan Lake, already alluded to, is the source from which proceed the beautiful Kauterskill Falls, represented above, as also the source of the Kauterskill River, which finds its way into the Hudson, at Catskill Village. The falls are situated about 2 miles from the Mountain House. Cooper, the novelist, in his novel of the "Pioneer," thus mentions them:—

"The water comes croaking and winding among the rocks, first, so slow that a trout might swim into it, then starting and running like any creature that wanted to make a fair spring, till it gets to where the mountain divides, like the cleft foot of a deer, leaving a deep hollow for the brook to tumble into. The first pitch is nigh 200 feet, and the water looks like flakes of snow before it touches the bottom, and then gathers itself together again for a new start; and maybe flutters over 50 feet of flat rock before it falls for another 100 feet, when it jumps from shelf to shelf, first running this way and that way, striving to get out of the hollow, till it finally gets to the plain."

VIEW DOWN SLEEPY HOLLOW—CATSKILL MOUNTAINS.

As another view of one of the cascades, we present one taken from the ledge of rocks, over which the water rushes silently but swiftly over the precipice, down into the beautiful gorge of "Sleepy Hollow."

The Fawn's Leap.—Such is the title given to the romantic scene represented by the annexed engraving. One can hardly imagine a more charming spot than this, when the ripe summer has dressed the trees in their green suits, and the gushing waters are swollen just enough to give impetuous force to their sweeping motion. This fascinating place is a favourite resort for poetic and reflective minds, who are sometimes detained here for hours together, as if charmed into inactivity and held in physical, if not mental, bondage by the exquisite beauty of the unequalled picture spread out before them.

THE FAWN'S LEAP.

Round Top.—This is the title of the highest peak on the Catskill Mountains, being 3,800 feet from the level of the river. The view from the summit of this acclivity is grand and beautiful beyond description.

High Peak is the second eminence in height, reaching to an altitude of 3,720 feet, and should be visited by all tourists.

Stony Clove is a wild mountain pass, situated about six miles from the Mountain House, but well worth a long walk to see.

Plauterkill Clove is another grand pass, five miles below the Kauterskill passage. A mountain torrent, combining all the sublime beauties of glen, rock and cascade, winds romantically through it.

The Mountain House, Catskill.—This is a large first-class hotel, resting near the edge of a precipitous cliff full 2,200 feet above the Hudson River, and from which a most magnificent view of the surrounding country is obtained; embracing not only the thriving villages which adorn either side of the Hudson, but commanding the distinct proportions of the long range of New England hills to the eastward. The site of this house is made interesting by the remark of old Leather-Stocking (in Cooper's "Pioneers,") who described it as a spot, 'whence creation might be seen at a single glance." Within a mile of the house is the place where Irving's "nappy" hero, *Rip Van Winkle*, had his famous sleep of fifteen years' duration.

The Laurel House is a small and very well-conducted hotel, situated close to the Falls, and overlooking the magnificent glen. This house is open all winter, and its charges are somewhat lower than at the other house.

Guides.—In order to see and enjoy all the beautiful sights as well as to learn their legendary history—none the less interesting if tinctured with fable—it is advisable that six or more tourists should club together, and engage a guide to conduct them to the various places of interest. Such a course will save much time, and introduce many novel sights that might be lost to the solitary stroller.

SARATOGA SPRINGS.

Where is the traveller of any pretensions in either Europe or America, who has not heard of this, the renowned Harrowgate of America? And where is the European who visits America for the first time, or the American tourist who has not spent, or does not intend to spend a few days at this most celebrated of all the inland watering places?

The British visitor will find life at Saratoga a repetition to a great extent of that at Harrowgate (England). At both, there are the mineral waters which visitors swallow both "fast and furious," without stint; the same large fountains or springs, where the grave, the gay, the lively and crippled all meet to quaff of one of nature's peculiar wines; the same large hotels which are similar in character and good cheer; the same pure and bracing air; the same pic-nics, pedestrian and driving excursions; the same early rising and going to bed late, after the identical "hop" has been indulged in, and where the same Cupid has probably been letting fly his darts. The picture of life at Saratoga and Harrowgate are almost identical, one of the most remarkable differences being the greater variety of character which one meets at the queen of American watering places, in men from all parts of the world, and with consequently greater peculiarities and marked characteristics. From the sunny South of Florida, to beyond the Banks of Newfoundland, will all the various types of American character be met with; and, of itself, not the least interesting subject for contemplation, by the physiognomist more particularly, when at Saratoga.

SARATOGA.

Above we present a faithful sketch of the town of Saratoga, with Congress Hall Hotel on the right, and Union Hotel immediately opposite to it.

SARATOGA LAKE.

The above sketch represents a beautiful sheet of water 9 miles long, 3 miles wide, situated about 3 1-2 miles from the Springs, and 8 miles west of the Hudson, into which its waters flow through the Fish Creek.

Saratoga Lake is visited by almost every sojourner at the Springs; the beauty of the lake, the change of scene it presents, the delicious fish which are there caught, and the delightful excursions made upon its waters, as well as amongst its woods, all conspire to render it one of the great attractions of Saratoga.

There are about twelve different springs in the neighborhood of Saratoga; but those chiefly resorted to are nine in number, of different names, the waters of some of them being as injurious as the others are beneficial in certain complaints.

The chief fountain is known by the name of Congress Spring, with an invariable temperature all the year round of fifty degrees Fahrenheit.

The hotels are numerous and unexceptionable, at from $2 to $2 50 (8s. to 10s.) per day, with numerous excellent boarding houses, at very reasonable charges.

The scenery of and around Saratoga does not call for special remark, being for the most part tame; yet several pleasant excursions may be made in the neighborhood, more particularly to the lake, noticed above.

Saratoga is situated 185 miles from the city of New York, and 239 miles from Boston, rail all the way. From New York proceed by rail, or steamboat, up the Hudson—"the Rhine of America"—to Albany, 146 miles, thence per rail, 39 miles, to Saratoga.

Tourists bound for Lake George from Saratoga proceed by the Troy and Whitehall Railroad for 15 miles to Moreau Station, thence by stage for other 15 miles on plank-road to Caldwell, the southern end of the lake. On the way thither, Glenn's Falls, 9 miles, and Bloody Pond, 4 miles from the lake, may be visited.

GLENN'S FALLS. The bold and rugged scenery of this place is in striking contrast with the tame and quiet country in and near Saratoga. The passage of the river is through a wild, romantic ravine and the writhing waters rush in a furious descent of 75 feet over a rocky precipice 900 feet in length. Cooper, in his "Last of the Mohicans," has chosen this neighbourhood as the scene of some of his most interesting chapters.

BLOODY POND. About midway between Glenn's Falls and the lake we pass a dark glen, in which lie the famous waters of *Bloody Pond*, and close by is *Williams' Rock*, marking the spot where fell Col. Williams in an engagement with the French and Indians in 1755. The slain in this sanguinary battle were carelessly thrown into the waters near by, since known as *Bloody Pond*.

LAKE GEORGE.

This is esteemed one of the most beautiful of the lesser lakes of America, and is situated near the eastern border of the State of New York, and empties its waters in a northerly direction into Lake Champlain. It lies north and south, is 36 miles long, and from 2 to 3 miles wide. Its elevation is near 250 miles above the Hudson River. The water is remarkably clear and transparent, the bottom being plainly seen at several fathoms depth. The scenery along its banks is extremely picturesque, and very pleasing to the lover of natural beauty. The lake is dotted over with numerous little islands of various forms and sizes, the number of which is stated by the popular voice to be equal to the number of days in a year. Many of these are respectable in size, and very fertile; others are diminutive and barren.

Fish, such as salmon-trout, silver-trout, brook-trout, perch, pike, etc., abound, and are of good size, and easily caught.

The Indian name of this lake is Horicon or the *Silvery Waters.* They also called it Caniderioit or the *tail of the lake*, in reference to its position near the southern termination of Lake Champlain. By the French it was named *Lac Sacrament*, signifying the purity of its waters. The first and the last names are really significant of the purity and clearness of this delightful lake, which is the more noticeable from the fact that all the other lakes on either side are more or less colored and impregnated with lime.

We annex a few sketches of the most beautiful portions of its scenery.

CALDWELL—LAKE GEORGE.

The above sketch represents the village of Caldwell, which is situated at the southern extremity of the lake, and near the ruins of the old fort. It is one of the most frequented points, although not the most retired in this charming district. The neighborhood of Toole's Inn, a few miles eastward, as well as Bolton and Garfield, will be found more secluded, and admirably adapted for angling pursuits, and where ample and excellent accommodation is to be met with.

Caldwell is a small village, containing a population of about 200, and several handsome private residences, two first-class hotels, two churches, court-house, jail, etc.

The ruins of Fort William Henry, which are close to the hotel of that name, were built by the British in 1755. A mile south-east are the ruins of Fort George.

LAKE GEORGE.

FROM CALDWELL.

The above illustration represents the pretty little steamer *Minnehaha* leaving the head waters of the lake, from which she proceeds to Ticonderoga—36 miles distant—at the other end of the lake, where she lands her passengers, gives ample time for a survey of that locality, and returns the same day to Caldwell. The trip is one which ought to be taken by all tourists; reminding one very much, in many respects, of the sail on Loch Katrine (Scotland), to whose beauties those of Lake George have been considered equal.

THE ISLANDS ON LAKE GEORGE.

During the course of the steamer up the lake, the tourist will have an opportunity of seeing the various islands which cover the face of the lake at particular points, leading us back to the recollection and a comparison when threading through amongst the Thousand islands on the noble St. Lawrence, or when passing up Loch Lomond, the Queen of the Scottish lakes.

We here quote the words of Addison Richards, an American writer, who says regarding this particular portion of the lake:

"With every changing hour—dawn, sunset and night—with the varying weather—from the calm of drowsy morning to the eve of gathering storm—these islands are found in ever-changing phases. As they sleep for a moment in the deep quiet of a passing cloud-shadow, you sigh for rest in their cooling bowers. Anon the sun breaks over them, and you are still as eager to mingle in their now wild and lawless revelry. You may shake up the lake like a kaleidoscope, seeing with every varying change a new picture by simply varying your relative position to these islands. Now you have a foreground of pebbly beach, or, perchance, of jagged rock, or of forest *debris*, with the spreading water and the distance-tinted hills to fill up the canvas; or, peeping beneath the pendent boughs of the beech and maple, an Arcadian bower discloses vistas of radiant beauty."

The islands, as passed, come in the following order:—

Diamond Island, near Durham Bay, once the scene of a sharp engagement between the troops of General Burgoyne's army and the Americans, in 1777.

Long Island, near Harris Bay, where Montcalm moored his bateaux in 1757.

Dome Island, where Putnam's troops bivouacked whilst he went to acquaint General Webb with the movements of the enemy.

Bolton, situated at the widest part of the lake. From the highest elevation in the vicinity extensive and magnificent views are obtained of Lake Champlain and surrounding country. Excellent sport for the rod and the gun is to be had there.

Tongue Mountain will now be reached, projecting considerably into the lake, with Black Mountain rising up behind it.

Shelving Rock, on the eastern shore, the pallisades of the lake, and

Fourteen Mile Island, situated in front of the last-mentioned rock.

The steamer now approaches the "Narrows," and to all appearance as if at the end of the delightful journey, but only to proceed with a change of scene which we now notice.

ENTRANCE TO THE NARROWS.

FROM THE SOUTH.

Almost the finest portion of the trip is when passing through the Narrows. At every turn the steamer takes in threading through the apparently mountain barriers, new views and scenes of beauty are presented to the eye. At one point, in passing one of the narrows, a broad expanse of lake opens up to view; a distant island is seen resting on its soft reflection in the calm water; beyond that is a neck of the main land, darkened by the shadow of a neighbouring hill; and, in the extreme distance, a massive mountain, raising its bold top into the clouds, and rendered soft, blue and indistinct by the intervening atmosphere; while several islets, clothed with rich verdure, shroud the foreground of the picture in deep, effective shadow. At other spots the prospect widens, revealing a sweep of the lake, studded with islands of various shape and size, whose verdure is tipped and streaked with flickering gleams of light.

Sabbath-Day Point.—The first place of interest after leaving the Narrows is the point made memorable by the landing of Gen. Abercrombie, who here sought refreshment and rest for his army on a bright Sabbath morning in 1758; hence the name of "Sabbath-Day Point." Two years before a small band of colonists had been attacked and defeated with great slaughter by a party of French and Indians. In 1776 this place was made a scene of strife between a body of Americans and a party of Tories with their Indian allies, which resulted in the defeat of the latter.

Rogers's Slide.—This place is named after a Major Rogers, who, while flying from a party of Indians in 1758, exhibited a specimen of what in our days would be called Yankee cunning, by changing his snow shoes from toe to heel so as to make his pursuers think he had walked over a huge precipice, when in fact he had slidden cautiously down to a lower point, and from thence to the ice below, where he snapped his fingers at his foe, and made good his escape. On the opposite side of the lake at this point is to be seen the precipice known as Anthony's Nose.

Prisoner's Island.—Two miles further on we come to the island which obtained its name from the circumstance of its having been used during the war as a place of confinement for prisoners taken by the English.

Howe's Landing.—The next point of interest is named after Gen. Howe, who was killed at the attack of Ticonderoga. The English, just previous to that event, landed their troops at this place, which lies near the foot of the lake, and terminates the list of interesting objects on the sheet of "silvery waters."

Fort Ticonderoga.—On leaving Lake George, a walk or ride of about four miles brings us to Fort Ticonderoga, which lies on the stream of water which connects Lake George with Lake Champlain. The fort, which in fact belongs to the last-mentioned lake, is made famous on account of its historical associations. It was originally erected by the French, in 1756, and being surrounded on three sides by water, and protected by a large swamp on the fourth side, it was considered a place of great strength.

In 1758, the English with 16,000 men under Gen. Abercrombie, attacked the fort, and for two days fought with a valour and perseverance deserving of success. But the impregnability of the place, and the constant fire of the garrison of 6,000 French from behind their impenetrable breastworks, were too much for the brave besiegers, who were obliged to retreat with a loss of 2,000 men, Lord Howe being among the first to fall.

In the following year, however, the fort was taken, with scarcely any resistance, by Gen. Amherst, and it remained in the hands of the English until the commencement of the Revolutionary war.

In 1775, Congress directed the famous and eccentric Ethan Allen to head his band of "Green Mountain boys" and take the fort, which duty Ethan accomplished without shedding a drop of blood. On reaching the shore opposite the fort, Allen happily procured the services of a boy named Nathan Beman, who was in the habit of playing in the fort, and was acquainted with every nook and corner in it. With his little guide, and 83 men, he crossed the stream, and being too impatient to wait for the rest of his troops, he determined to attack the enemy with the force he had. After making a brief but inspiring speech to his men, he led them rapidly up the heights. It was just at the dawn of day, and so cautious and silent had been the march that, on arriving at the gates, they were found wide open, and the first intimation the sentinels had of the presence of the foe, was the sight of Allen and his men walking into the barrack-yard. After securing the astonished guards, Allen drew up his men on the parade ground, who announced their presence to the sleepy garrison by giving three hearty cheers. Allen then hastened to the room of the commandant, and demanded the immediate surrender of the fort. The astonished commandant, springing from his bed and rubbing his eyes, as if bewildered by a dream, asked by what authority such a preposterous demand was made. "By authority from the Great Jehovah and the Continental Congress," was Allen's cool reply. Seeing the uselessness of defence against a resolute and armed body of men backed by such high authority, the commandant immediately surrendered, and with his garrison of fifty men were soon after forwarded to Hartford as prisoners of war. The fort was subsequently taken by the English under Burgoyne, and held to the close of the war.

LAKE CHAMPLAIN.

There is probably no lake in America, which, in the beautiful variety of its scenery, and in historical interest, can compare favourably with Lake Champlain. As our limits will not permit a complete description of this famous Lake, we must be content to point out such of the principal objects of interest as will be of most value to the tourist or to the general reader.

Lake Champlain runs nearly north and south, and is 120 miles in length; its breadth varying from one-fourth of a mile to 13 miles, covering an area of 500 miles. Its waters are well stored with all the varieties of fish usually found in the larger lakes. The lake was discovered in 1609, by Samuel Champlain, the founder of Quebec, who, after a bloody conquest of a body of Iroquois Indians whom he met on its banks, took formal possession, and baptized it with his own name. The lake is connected with the Hudson River by the Champlain canal, which is 64 miles long and 40 feet wide, and was constructed at the cost of over $1,000,000. It also connects with the St. Lawrence and Montreal by railroad and canal.

Whitehall.—This is the starting-point from the head of the lake by such travellers as come from Albany by rail, and is a thriving, busy town of some 4 or 5,000 inhabitants. Steamers, during the travelling season, daily leave this place for a voyage up the lakes, and, touching at Benson, 13 miles distant, and Orville, 7 miles further, reach, at the twenty-fourth mile Fort Ticonderoga, where passengers from Lake George are taken on board, and commence the voyage up the wider part of the lake.

Crown Point.—During the Revolution, the English had a fort at this place, which was surprised and taken by a detachment of "Green Mountain Boys," under Seth Warner, on the same day on which Ethan Allen took Ticonderoga.

Chimney Point is on the opposite shore, and obtained its name from the fact that a number of chimneys once belonging to the old French huts, were found standing after the place was abandoned in 1759. The lake at this point is half a mile wide.

Westport is 16 miles from Crown Point, on the east side of the lake. A pretty village of 1,000 inhabitants, having a ferry to the opposite shore of Vermont.

Fort Cassin.—This is a small village on the Vermont side, and was formerly a landing-place for Vergennes passengers, who now stop at Basin Harbour, opposite Westport. This place is remarkable as having been the point where Commodore McDonough, in 1814, fitted out the fleet with which he gained his memorable victory over the English in the same year. The place is named after Lieut. Cassin of the American navy, who, with 200 men, gallantly and successfully repulsed a large body of English, who attempted to destroy the American fleet, while getting ready for sea.

Split Rock is one of the greatest curiosities of the lake. It is an immense mass of rock, about half an acre in extent, and 30 feet above the water, and has been detached by some convulsion of nature from the neighbouring cliff, from which it is separated about 12 feet. A little south of this rock a light-house has been erected.

Four Brothers are four small islands, on which, in consequence of their lying out of the line of passage, and therefore being undisturbed, large quantities of gulls delight to congregate.

Juniper Island, four miles further on, has precipitous banks of slate rock over thirty feet high. A light-house was erected here in 1826.

Rock Dundee next appears, rising from the water to a height of 30 feet; and close to it is *Pottier's Point* at the mouth of Shelburne Bay.

Burlington.—This is one of the largest and handsomest towns in Vermont, and forms a centre for several lines of railway, steamboat and stage-coach communication. It is 25 miles from Plattsburg, and 50 from Rouse's Point, and contains about 10,000 inhabitants. The position of the town is very fine, and many of its buildings really beautiful, particularly that of the *University of Vermont,* which was founded in 1791. Twenty miles north-east of the town, *Mount Mansfield* rises to a height of 4,279 feet, and at about the same distance on the south-east the *Camel's Hump* lifts up its back to an elevation of 4,183 feet. Both are plainly seen from the lake.

Winooski, Port Kent and Trembleu Point, are small, but thriving villages, which lie along the route, the former in Vermont, and the two last in New York.

Ausable River flows into the lake a little north of Port Kent. There are several beautiful falls on this river. The one called the *Chasm,* 2 miles back of the lake, falls through a ravine of singular magnificence. The rocks rise perpendicularly from 80 to 150 feet on either side of the river, for the distance of 2 miles, and with an average width of 50 feet.

Port Jackson.—This place is celebrated as being near the scene of a severe naval engagement between the English and American fleets, in 1776. The Americans were defeated, and running their ships on shore, the men escaped, and left their vessels to be burned by the enemy.

Plattsbury.—This is a thriving town of 4,000 inhabitants, and is used as a national military post. The government have erected extensive barracks here. It was near this town that the American and British fleets and armies met on water and on land, and entered into deadly conflict in September, 1814. On the lake the action continued for two and a half hours, and resulted in the striking of the British flag. The enemy on shore, beholding the result on the lake, became disheartened and confused, and soon retreated, leaving the Americans masters of the field and lake.

Rouse's Point.—Passing a few picturesque islands and one or two small villages, the voyager comes to *Rouse's Point,* which is the last stopping-place within the United States, being 125 miles from Whitehall. Railways from the Eastern States connect here with lines to Montreal. Passengers may take the cars here for Montreal, or, if they choose, continue their voyage to St. Johns, which lies at the head of navigation on the lake. If the latter course is chosen, the only objects worthy of especial notice on the route is *Ash Island,* at the mouth of Richelieu River; *La Colle,* a British military post; *Isle aux Noix,* a British frontier post, now occupied by British troops, and commanding the channel of the river; *Aulburg,* a small village on the Vermont side, and Highgate, 17 miles above Rouse's Point, and which is a favourite place of resort during the summer months, on account of the excellent springs which abound here, and for its hunting and fishing advantages.

If the passage on Lake Champlain be made on a pleasant, calm day, the voyager will discover a thousand beauties during his journey over this beautiful route, which cannot be described in books or written with the pen.

ALEX. HARTHILL & Co., *Steam Printers,* 20 *North William St., New York*

Interior View of F. DERBY & COMP'Y'S Fashionable Custom Tailoring Establishment,

57 WALKER STREET, NEW YORK.

Special Notice.

F. DERBY & COMPANY

HAVE THE GOOD FORTUNE

To announce that they have received, and have now in Store, a complete assortment of New Goods, being made to order for their Fall and Winter Sales, through

Messrs. BARLOW, PAYNE & CO.,

(Manufacturers' Agents, London, England.)

Adapted to the wants of GENTLEMEN OF TASTE who appreciate style and quality in Clothing.

MERCHANT TAILORS AND IMPORTERS,

57 Walker Street, New York.

NEW YORK.

In our description of the great city of the western world, we shall avoid, as far as possible, all statistical matter, regarding which ample information may be had in works exclusively devoted to such details. We prefer giving a brief account of the city from the earliest to the present time, and, with the views given of its magnificent streets and buildings, we hope to

VIEW OF THE CITY OF NEW YORK.

FROM BROOKLYN, LONG ISLAND.

convey to our readers at a distance, an idea of its importance as the most populous city on the whole continent of America. As may be known by many, New York was discovered in 1609, by an Englishman named Henry Hudson, at that time in the service of the Dutch—and in 1613, the settlement of the Island was commenced, under the title of New Amsterdam. In 1621, a

Dutch West India company commenced operations upon it, and in 1626, purchased the whole island from the Indians (the Manhattans) for the paltry sum of $25, (£5 stg.) the exports alone that year amounting to $1900. It was thus held till 1664, when it was taken by the English. Charles the 2d, then king, changed its name to that of New York, in honour of James the 2d, who then bore the title of Duke of York and Albany. In 1686, James the 2d, then king, abolished the representative system, and, as affording one of the numerous proofs of his kingly bigotry, took it into his head to prohibit the use of the printing-press.

It was retaken from the English by the Dutch in 1673, retaken again in 1674 by the English, and held by them till the Revolutionary period of 1776-1783, when it was finally evacuated by the British army, thus ending British rule on the 25th November, 1783. In 1812-13, another war broke out between Great Britain and America, but not leading to New York changing hands once more. Notwithstanding, therefore, wars, fevers, fires, great commercial disasters, cholera, etc., etc., the city has gone on progressively, from a population of 23,614 in 1786, to upwards of 600,000 in 1859.

New York is situated upon what is called Manhattan Island—a strip of land 13¼ miles long, by one mile and three-fifths average width. Greatest breadth, at 83d street, is two miles and one-third. In all, about 22 square miles, or 14,000 acres. It rises gradually above the level of the water around the sides, whilst the greater part of it is level, or been rendered so. It is very compactly built upon for about 5 miles, in straight lines from the point at the Battery end of it. The streets, for the most part, are laid out in a convenient and easily understood plan. The streets commencing at Houston street, (one mile from the City Hall,) are classed into 14 regular "avenues," as they are called, which are crossed at right angles by 156 streets, numerically designated. Some of the streets are crooked and narrow, but generally speaking, they are wide and spacious—ranging from 60 to 120 feet wide. The greatest fault a stranger is likely to find with the streets is the filthy state the most of them are in—as if there were neither scavengers nor paviours in the city.

New York is bounded on the north by the Harlem River—which separates Manhattan Island from the main land; on the east by the East River, which separates it from Long Island; on the south by the harbour, and on the west by the North, or Hudson River, which separates it from New Jersey.

The width of the East River is from one-third to half a mile, and that of the North River from 1 to 1¼ miles.

Navigation is open throughout all the year. There can be no doubt but that the harbour of New York is one of the most beautiful in the world—presenting one of the finest spectacles on a fine day—with its piers crowded with ships of all nations—the numbers of clean-looking steamers passing up and down, and the beauty of the scenery on the opposite shores, and on every side.

The defences are placed at the Narrows—on Long Island side, and on Staten Island—and in the East River at Throg's Neck; whilst within the harbour are batteries on Bedloe's and Ellis Islands, Governor's Island, Castle William, and South Battery—commanding every point of entrance. We may safely say, that nearly every branch of manufactures is carried on in New York, excepting in the great items of cotton and wool—whilst its commerce extends to every corner of the American continent, as well as all over the world, wherever the natural products of the earth, or manufactures, are to be bought, sold, or exchanged. The public buildings are very numerous. We annex a list elsewhere, together with engravings of a few of the principal ones, together with a list of such places of interest and amusement as the stranger will be pleased in visiting.

The streets where the private residences are, are elegant in the extreme. We allude more particularly to such as 4th and 5th Avenues, and Union and Madison Squares, where the most stately mansions will be found, finished off in first-rate style, mostly built of a brown-coloured stone. In summer, with the rows of trees along each side of the streets, their fine appearance will at once attract the admiration of the stranger.

The principal street for bankers, insurance offices, etc., is Wall street—the Lombard street of America.

For wholesale dry goods stores—Pearl, William, Broad, Pine, Cedar, Liberty streets, College Place, and Vesey street.

For wholesale grocers, and commission and shipping merchants—Water and Front streets.

For heavy dry goods and variety stores, Grand and Catharine streets.

For hardware—Beekman, Platt, John and Pearl streets.

For booksellers and publishers, binderies, etc.—Nassau and William Streets.

For Jewellers—Maiden lane, Courtland street, and Broadway.

For boot and shoe materials, Ferry, Jacob, and Gold streets.

Whilst Broadway, like Cheapside in London, contains an *omnium gatherum* of all sorts—from the selling of a cup of coffee in a restaurant, to a ship load of "Yankee notions."

The wharves extending all round New York nearly—the vessels placed with their bows all pointing towards the city, and so situated very conveniently for loading and unloading, and when ready for sea, have only to drop into the stream and are carried down and out to sea, the magnificent river and bay having few obstructions in the shape of bars, etc.

The stranger, however, who has been accustomed to look at the shipping in the stupendous docks of London and Liverpool, will at once discover the poor accommodation New York affords in comparison with the facilities afforded for the harbouring or dockage of vessels in Great Britain. Notwithstanding this, however, the immense shipping business of the port of New York is carried on somehow—the ingenuity of the Americans finding ways and means to clear their vessels with promptitude and ease.

Broadway is the great main artery of the city, through which people, omnibuses, wagons, and carriages, rush in one incessant stream, surging backward and forward, from the earliest hour in the morning, to the latest hour at night.

A walk along Broadway will disclose pictures of society—men and things, in all conceivable variations and degrees. There, the slouching "loafer" will be seen, close to the "Broadway swell"—the successful miner, just arrived from the Californian diggings, alongside of the wealthiest and most handsomely dressed lady in New York, who is out for her walk on that great "vanity fair"—the newly-arrived emigrant from Great Britain, as he goes gaping along at what he sees, whilst he is almost stupefied with the bustle and confusion around him. It is entirely different from any one of the great thoroughfares of London, whilst it com-

BROADWAY, NEW YORK.

bines the features of all—the bustle and throng of Cheapside, in its incessant stream of omnibuses and vehicles of all sorts—of Regent street, with its fashionable promenade and *bon ton* of society—of Oxford street and Holborn, with middle-class stores, as well as elegant warehouses, including the exclusively wholesale stores of a St. Paul's church-yard, as well.

"The other chief artery of the city is that of the Bowery—partaking very much of Holborn, with a mixture of the Whitechapel of London—where a large amount of retail business is transacted.

"THE CITY HALL OF NEW YORK—from its central position, and classic marble frontage—is one of the finest and most prominent buildings in the city. The front and two ends are of white marble, and the back, which is never shone upon by the sun, of brown sandstone. The City Hall contains a gallery of historical art, invaluable to the lover of Knickerbocker times. In the Governor's Room, enjoyed by the public only on reception days, are the portraits of all the governors of the State, from the time of Lewis, and of the mayors of the city, with several of the presidents, painted by artists of national reputation. There may be seen Henry Hudson, Columbus, and hosts of other worthies, while the archives of the city contain a vast amount of information of great interest to the historian. Besides the rooms of the aldermen and common council, there was in former times a noble banqueting hall for the city magnates."

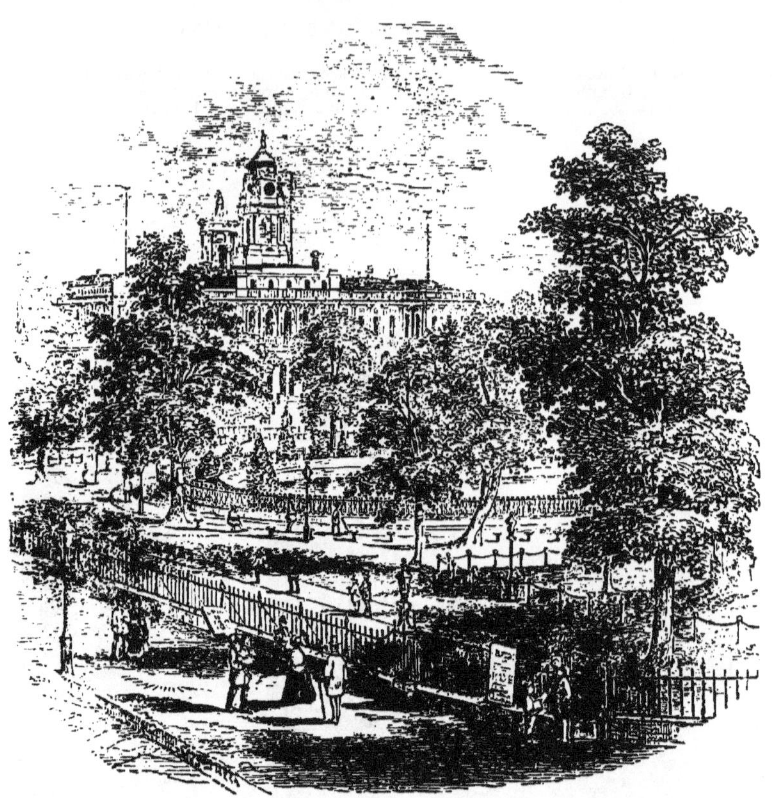

THE PARK AND CITY HALL, NEW YORK.

Adjacent to the City Hall is the old Debtor's Prison, now the Hall of Records, the old Alms House, entirely appropriated to governmental use.

In the Park are held public meetings, and in front of the City Hall are planted cannon, which are fired by the respective political parties, on the achievement of any party victory, as well as on other general public rejoicings. The Park forms a great resort for the citizens, and in the hot months of summer, forms, by its trees, a delightful shady retreat.

Last year, the City Hall took fire, and a large portion of the upper part of it was destroyed. It is now being re-built, however.

The New York University, situated between Washington Place and Waverly Place, fronts Washington Square towards the west, forming a noble ornament to the city, being built of Westchester marble, and exhibits a specimen of the English collegiate style of architecture.

The building is 180 feet long, and 100 wide. It was founded in 1831.

"In front, this oblong is divided into five parts —a central building, with wings flanked by towers, one rising on each of the four corners of the edifice. This central building or chapel is superior to the rest in breadth, height, and character, and is somewhat similar to that of King's College, Cambridge, England—a masterpiece of pointed architecture, and a model for succeeding ages. It is 55 feet broad, and 85 feet deep, including the octangular turrets, one of which rises at each of the four corners. The two ends are gabled, and are, as well as the sides, crowned with an embattled parapet. The chapel receives its principal light from a window in the western end. This window is 24 feet wide, and 50 high. From the central building, or chapel, wings project right and left, the windows of which have square heads, with two lights, a plain transom, and the upper division trefoiled. The principal entrance is under the great western window. The doors are of oak, richly panelled, and filled with tracery of open work, closely studded with bronze.

"The institution has a chancellor and eleven professors. It has in its collegiate department 150 students, and a valuable library and philosophical apparatus. Connected with it is an extensive grammar school, and a flourishing medical department. The whole number of students is about 700. Commencement, third Monday in July. (See next page for engraving.)

UNIVERSITY, NEW YORK.

"The chapel is probably the most beautiful room of the kind in America. It is open to the public, on Sundays, for religious worship. The Library and rooms of the New York Historical Society are in the building. The building is accessible to the visitor at all times."

"THE TOMBS occupy the space between Centre, Elm, Leonard and Franklin streets, the site of an old filthy pond, which had its outlet through Canal street. The Halls of Justice is a much-admired specimen of modernized Egyptian architecture. It is built of light granite from Hallowell, Maine. It is 253 feet long, and 200 wide, and occupies the four sides of a hollow square, with a large centre building within the area. The front is approached by eight steps, leading to a portico of four massive Egyptian columns. The windows, which extend to the height of two stories, have massive iron grated frames, surmounted with cornices, ornamented with a winged globe and serpents. The two fronts on Leonard and Franklin streets have each two entrances, with two massive columns each. The gloomy aspect of this building has won for it the general name of "The Tombs." It is occupied by the Court of Sessions, a police court, and some other court-rooms, besides a prison for male and female offenders awaiting trial. The open court within the walls is used as a place of execution for State criminals.

Persons can gain admittance on application for a written permit, at the keeper's room, between 10, A. M. and 3, P. M."

In the fore-ground of the view will be seen one of the "City Railroad Cars," noticed elsewhere.

CUSTOM HOUSE.—The lower engraving on the following page, represents the Custom House of New York, situated at the corner of Nassau and Wall streets.

"The Custom House has the form and solidity of a Greek temple, and is as enduring as the pyramids. The edifice, of white marble, is 200 feet long, by 90 in width, and 80 feet high. Some of the blocks weigh 30 tons. The two fronts have 8 Doric columns, nearly 6 feet in diameter; the sides, 16 heavy pilasters. A flight of 18 steps from Wall street, brings the visitor to the main entrance. The Rotunda is 60 feet in diameter, and the dome, under which the four deputy collectors have desks, is supported in part by 16 Corinthian pillars. In the little room of the treasurer, near at hand, is received two-thirds of the revenue of the country. The Custom House was erected between the

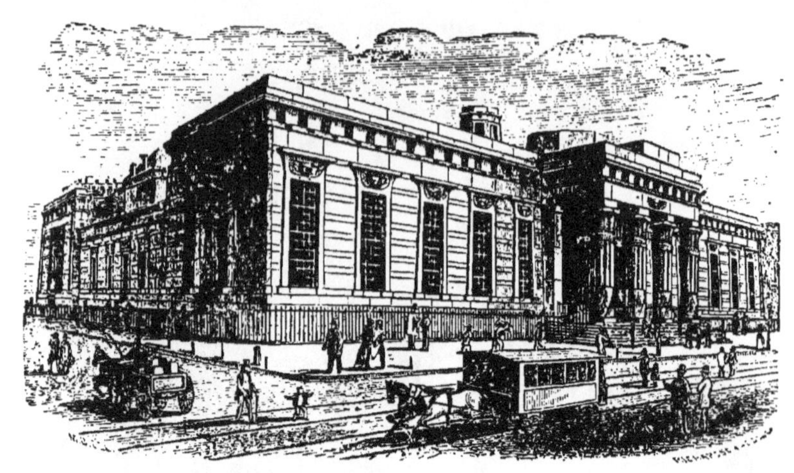

HALLS OF JUSTICE, OR THE TOMBS, NEW YORK.

CUSTOM-HOUSE, WALL STREET, NEW YORK.

MERCHANTS' EXCHANGE, WALL STREET, NEW YORK.

years 1834–1841, and cost, including the lot, $1,195,000."

The amount of accommodation provided for the transactions of the Custom House, appears to be totally inadequate to the immense amount of business furnished by the port.

MERCHANTS' EXCHANGE.—The above engraving represents one of the most beautiful and costly buildings in America, and surpassing any other in the city in size and solidity of construction. "It occupies a whole square of ground, and has a front of 200 feet on Wall street, with an average depth of 160 feet; is 5 stories high, including the basement, and fire-proof throughout, the floors and roof being entirely of masonry and metal. The principal material is brick-faced, with massive blocks of granite, chiefly from the inexhaustible quarries of Quincy, Massachusetts. The most remarkable features of this huge building are its graceful portico, presenting to the eye a facade of 18 Ionic columns, each nearly 40 feet in height, and upwards of 4 feet in diameter, the shafts of which are each a single stone (wrought in the most perfect manner, at a cost of $3000,) and the Rotunda, or Exchange Room, which is 100 feet in diameter, with a double dome of brick, surmounted by a vertical sky-light, with movable sashel, which allows thorough and complete ventilation. The dome is supported partly by 8 massive Corinthian columns of Italian marble, weighing 41 tons each, in very large sections, imported expressly for the purpose." The floor is flagged with the same material, and altogether the room is one of the finest in America.

THE FREE ACADEMY, NEW YORK.

"THE FREE ACADEMY is on Lexington avenue, corner of Twenty-third street, and may easily be reached by taking a Broadway and Fourth avenue omnibus, or the Harlem rail-cars, opposite the Astor House. The building is 80 feet wide, by 125 feet deep, and is intended to accommodate 1,000 pupils. It is in the style of the town-halls of the Netherlands, and is well adapted for its purpose, besides being a conspicuous ornament to the upper part of the city.

The cost of the ground was $87,510, of the building, $75,000, while the various appliances of apparatus and furniture have cost $26,567. The only requisites for admission are a knowledge of the branches taught in the public schools; it being also required that the applicant should have been a pupil in one of these schools for at least one year."

PRIVATE RESIDENCE.—(Corner of 5th Avenue and 34th Street, New York

PETER COOPER INSTITUTE, NEW YORK.

NEW YORK HOSPITAL, BROADWAY.

On the preceding page we give an illustration of a private residence in one of the principal streets in New York, viz., the Fifth avenue. In this street may be seen some of the largest and handsomest of the private residences of the New York merchants.

In summer, when the trees which line each side of the avenue are in full bloom, the street then has all the appearance of a beautiful grove.

The subject of the illustration in question forms one of the handsomest residences in the avenue, and in general architectural outline, compares favorably with any of the handsome mansions in the same locality. The architect is Mr. J. Sexton, of 121 Nassau street, New York.

The Cooper Institute.—This institution deserves a place among our illustrations of public buildings of the city, not only on account of the magnificence of the edifice, as a building, but as a memento of a most princely act on the part of a New York merchant—Mr. Peter Cooper—who, out of his wealth, has built this house with the view of founding an institution to be called "The Union," for the moral, social, and physical improvement of the youth, not only belonging to the City, or State, but of any part of the world. The sum donated to such a noble purpose, amounts to $300,000 (£60,000 stg.).

"The building is in Astor Place, opposite the new Bible House. The edifice is six stories high, occupying a space equal in extent to eight full lots, each 25 feet by 100, or 20,000 square feet. In the basement is a commodious lecture-room, 125 feet long, and in the upper story an observatory. The Union provides free courses of lectures, a free library, rooms for debating and other societies, and an office for the benefit of persons seeking literary employment, where their names and wishes may be registered, and application for their services received.

"The School of Design, for females, have rooms in this building, amply supplied with the materials for instruction."

The New York Hospital is one of the principal benevolent institutions of New York, which the stranger, as he walks along Broadway, cannot fail to notice.

"Situated on Broadway, fronting Wall street, with its portals invitingly open every day in the year, stands Trinity Church, a beautiful temple of worship. It is the third edifice of the kind erected upon the spot, the first having been destroyed in the great fire of 1776. The entire length of the building is 180 feet, of which 45 are due to the chancel. Width of nave, 54 feet; of chancel, 38 feet. Height to eaves, 50 feet, and to ridge, 90 feet, with a fine open roof. The inside walls of the church are of Caen stone, brought from Normandy in France—a material of an agreeable colour, and easily worked, being soft enough to be cut with a saw or knife. The windows are of richly stained glass; the ceilings painted blue, and the roof timbers covered with polychromatic decorations. The floors are tiled throughout, with tasteful ornamental patterns in chancel. The building will seat about 800, its cost having been $260,000. The architect of this splendid church is Mr. Upjohn, a celebrated Scotch architect.

"The lofty spire of the church is the Pompey's Pillar of New York—the most prominent object that first arrests the attention of the stranger, as he approaches the city from the Atlantic. The view from the top of the spire is without doubt the finest to be had in the city."

TRINITY CHURCH, BROADWAY, NEW YORK.

This magnificent building, recently erected, is remarkable for its peculiar architecture—being built in the style of many of the Italian churches of the middle ages—of brick, and cream-coloured stone, alternately.

Adjoining the church is the parsonage, situated on Twentieth street. Included in the design for this church, is the magnificent spire, or campanile, 300 feet high, the foundation only of it being at present built.

The church, inside, is fitted up elegantly and most comfortably, in small and large pews, to suit the families of members. The peculiar hue of the paint on the walls, the magnificently stained glass windows, partially obscured by a huge arch, facing the equally grand-looking, and powerful organ in the gallery opposite, the light streaming down from the cupola, behind the pulpit—the well-planned position the congregation occupy for seeing and hearing—the rich and gay dresses of the vast crowd of hearers—form altogether a *coup d' Œil* seldom to be met with.

This handsome edifice belongs to one of the Unitarian congregations of New York, over which the Rev Dr. Bellows is pastor.

It has cost already $170,000, including the parsonage. The campanile is estimated to cost $40,000; so that when it is completed, the whole edifice will have cost the large sum of $210,000, (£42,000 stg.).

The architect is Mr. Jacob Wrey Mould.

It is situated on the Fourth Avenue, near to Union Square—one of the most beautiful localities in the city. The cars which start from *opposite* the Astor House, pass the entrance to the church.

THE CHURCH OF ALL SOULS—NEW YORK.

THE MERCANTILE LIBRARY.—One of the finest and most useful institutions in New York, is the library and reading room of the Mercantile Library Association, situated at Clinton Hall, Astor Place, a little way out of Broadway (west end). The reading room is a magnificent apartment, equal to the reading rooms of the clubs in London and elsewhere. It is attended by a young lady waitress. There is a branch office in the city, for the convenience of parties residing in Brooklyn and places adjacent—where orders for books are received and delivered. From a report we quote :—

"The Library now contains 30,000 volumes, is rich in every popular and scientific department, and is catalogued to the end of the year 1856. Nearly 75,000 volumes were delivered to members in 1856. More than 20,000 of these were distributed through the branch office, at No. 16 Nassau street. The reading rooms are the most extensive in the United States, and contain nearly 300 magazines and newspapers selected from all parts of the world, full files of all the principal newspapers from their commencement, and a large number of books of reference. There are, beside, classes in various branches, and lectures in the winter, all for $2 a year."

Its members number upwards of 4,500.
In the vicinity is situated the well-known

ASTOR LIBRARY—named after Mr. Jacob Astor, one of the most successful and wealthy merchants of New York, who has bequeathed this splendid legacy as a *free* library, for the use of the citizens of the city, where he amassed a large fortune, although he entered the city—as it is said—a poor boy.

We find from a recent report of the librarian, that the fund invested for carrying on the institution yields about $13,000 a year, of which $7,000 goes for expenses, leaving $6,000 for books. More than 20,000 volumes have been added since 1854, including some exceedingly rare and valuable books.

During the day, it is frequented by many whose time and opportunities permit visiting it. As a free library, however, we confess we felt disappointed at finding that it is shut one hour after sunset—the only time when so many citizens have it in their power to frequent such an institution, and, of course, to thousands it must prove of no use whatever.

It is most comfortably, and even gorgeously fitted up, and for all who can attend during the day, it must prove a great boon.

POST-OFFICE, NASSAU STREET, BETWEEN CEDAR AND LIBERTY STREETS.—The whole business correspondence of this immense city, and through which passes the entire foreign correspondence of the United States and Canada—is conducted in this miserable shanty-looking building, which appears to us to be a disgrace to a country village—far less a city like New York. It has been, successively, a Dutch church, a riding-school, a prison, and an hospital. It is worthy of a visit, if only to see such a glaring instance of neglect, connected with so important a matter as a proper establishment fit for conducting the postal business of this great city, and which ought to be an honour to the city instead of one of its monuments of neglect, or stupidity—we know not which.

THE NEW ARSENAL.—Noticed elsewhere.

HIGH BRIDGE.—Harlem, 1400 feet long (see engraving).

CASTLE GARDEN EMIGRATION DEPOT.—At the Battery, east end of Broadway. (See notice of it elsewhere.)

NAVAL DRY DOCK.—Navy Yard, Brooklyn, said to be the largest in the world—built in ten years, at a cost of $2,150,000. Docks the largest ship in 4 hours 20 m.

Amongst the finest churches in the city, we may mention—

ALL SOUL'S CHURCH.—4th Avenue—Unitarian. (See engraving and notice elsewhere.)

TRINITY CHURCH.—Broadway, fronting Wall Street—Episcopal. The nearest approach to a cathedral in New York, about 200 feet long by 80 wide, in the florid Gothic style, with a very beautiful tower and spire, 284 feet high, containing a visitor's "view-point" of 250 feet in height. (See engraving.)

ST. PAUL'S CHAPEL.—Broadway, between Fulton and Vesey streets—Episcopal.

GRACE CHURCH.—Broadway, above Tenth s. —Episcopal.

ST. PATRICK'S CATHEDRAL.—Corner of Prince and Mott—Roman Catholic. 136 feet by 80, accommodating 2000 persons—Byzantine style.

FOURTH UNIVERSALIST CHURCH—Broadway, above Spring. Remarkable for the exquisite Gothic tracery of its carved wood-work, especially on the pulpit and canopy.

THE GREAT SYNAGOGUE.—Greene street, near Houston—Hebrew.

BENEVOLENT INSTITUTIONS.

NEW YORK HOSPITAL.—Broadway. (See engraving.)

BLIND ASYLUM.—9th avenue, near 33d street. A massive Gothic structure, covering one entire block. About 100 pupils are educated and taught appropriate trades.

DEAF AND DUMB INSTITUTION.—4th avenue and 50th street, on Washington Heights, covering 37 acres. About 250 mutes educated and taught trades.

ORPHAN ASYLUM.—Bloomingdale, near 80th st. 200 inmates.

EDUCATIONAL INSTITUTIONS.

NEW YORK UNIVERSITY.—Washington Sq. A noble marble building, with a beautiful chapel—mediæval Gothic. (See engraving.)

COLUMBIA COLLEGE.—Park Place, near Broadway. A president, 10 professors, and 150 students.

FREE ACADEMY.—Corner Lexington avenue and 23d street. (See engraving.)

UNION THEOLOGICAL SEMINARY.—University Place, near Washington Square. Six professors—100 students.

BIBLE HOUSE.—An immense building, occupying one entire triangular block, near the junction of 3d and 4th avenues, with a frontage of 700 feet.

General Theological Seminary.—20th st., corner 9th avenue—Episcopal.

University Medical School.—14th street, near 3d avenue. Extensive and well-arranged apparatus.

College of Physicians and Surgeons.—4th avenue, corner 23d street—Medical Museum.

New York Medical College.—East 13th street. Five months' course. Pathological Museum, and Laboratory for the practical study of Analytical Chemistry.

SCIENTIFIC AND LITERARY INSTITUTIONS.

American Institute.—349 Broadway. For the general advancement and *application* of science. Admission free. Holds an Annual Fair at Crystal Palace, and a Cattle Show.

Mechanics' Institute.—20 4th avenue. Gives popular scientific lectures. Mechanical Museum and reading-room—schools attached.

Cooper "Union."—Astor Place, opposite Bible House. Built by Peter Cooper, Esq. Free lectures, library, observatory, debating rooms, and literary employment office. (See engraving.)

New York Society Library.—University Place, near 12th street—36,000 volumes—visitors admitted.

Lyceum of Natural History.—14th street, near 4th avenue. Appropriate library and cabinet.

New York Law Institute.—City Hall. Very complete collection of 4500 volumes.

New York Historical Society.—University Building—20,000 volumes, cabinet of coins, etc.

Apprentices' Library.—Mechanics' Hall, Broadway, near Grand street—40,000 volumes.

FINE ART INSTITUTIONS.

National Academy of Design.—58 East 13th street. Spring exhibition of the works of living artists only. Much resorted to.

Dusseldorf Gallery.—548 Broadway. Good collection of the Flemish and German schools.

Bryan Gallery.—Corner Broadway and 13th street. Some fair originals and excellent copies.

PUBLIC BUILDINGS.

City Hall and Park.—(See engraving.)

Custom House.—Corner Wall and Nassau. An exquisitely pure Doric building of white marble, modelled from the Parthenon. (See engraving.) Admission free.

Merchants' Exchange.—Wall street. Elegant Ionic exterior. (See engraving.)

Halls of Justice.—Centre Street—popularly known as the "*Tombs.*" (See engraving.)

RAILROAD STATIONS IN NEW YORK.

Hudson River Railroad.—Depots: corner Warren street and College Place; Canal street, near Washington; West street, near Christopher; Thirty-First street, between Tenth and Eleventh avenues.

The time is marked for Thirty-First street depot—difference from others, 25 to 30 minutes.

Long Island Railroad.—Depot: foot of Atlantic street, Brooklyn.

New Jersey Railroad.—Depot: foot of Courtlandt street.

New York and Erie Railroad.—Depot: West street, foot of Duane street.

New Jersey Central and Steamboat Line.—Office—69 Wall street.

PUBLIC BUILDINGS.

Post-office, (Nassau street.)—Proceed to 146 Broadway, and east through Liberty street.

Custom House, (Nassau, corner Wall street.)—Proceed to 86 Broadway, and east in Wall street. (See engraving.)

Assay Office, (Wall street.)—Proceed as above for Custom House.

Merchants' Exchange, (Wall, corner William street.)—Proceed as above. (See engraving.)

City Hall, (in the Park.)—Proceed in Broadway to 260, and east in the Park. (See engraving.)

Board of Education Rooms (Grand, corner Elm street).—Proceed to 458 Broadway, and east in Grand street.

Free Academy, (23d street and Lexington avenue.)—Take a 3d or 4th avenue car to 23d street The Academy is located between those avenues. [See engraving.]

PUBLIC MARKETS.

Fulton, (South and Fulton streets.)—Proceed in Broadway to No. 208, and east in Fulton street to the river.

Catharine, (South and Catharine streets.)—Proceed in Broadway to No. 222, and east in Park Row, Chatham street, and East Broadway to No. 15, and southeast in Catharine street to the river.

Washington, (Fulton and West streets.)—Proceed in Broadway to No. 207, and west in Fulton street to the river.

Centre, (Grand and Centre streets.)—Proceed to No. 458 Broadway, and east in Grand street to No. 162.

Essex, (Grand and Essex streets.)—Proceed in Broadway to No. 458, and east in Grand street to No. 334.

Tompkins, (Bowery and 6th street.)—Proceed to 698 Broadway, east in 4th street to No. 394, and north in Bowery to No. 395.

Jefferson, (6th and Greenwich avenues.)—Proceed to No. 769 Broadway, and west in 9th street to No. 1.

Spring Street, (West and Spring streets.)—Proceed to 527 Broadway, and west in Spring street to the river.

Houston Street, (Pitt and Houston streets.)—Proceed in Broadway to No. 608, and east in Houston street to 174.

PUBLIC PARKS.

Battery, (Foot of Broadway.)—Proceed to No. 1 Broadway, and cross Battery Place.

Park, (corner Chambers street and Broadway.)—Proceed to 271 Broadway.

Washington, (Fourth and Wooster streets.)—Proceed to 698 Broadway, and west to Wooster street.

Union, (14th street.)—Proceed in Broadway to No. 862.

Madison, (23d street.)—Proceed in Broadway to No. 948.

Tompkins, (Avenue A.)—Proceed in Broadway to No. 754, and east in Eighth street.

Central, (59th street.)—Proceed in Broadway to its junction with 8th avenue—or take a 2d, 3d, or 4th avenue car to 86th street, and proceed west.

PLEASANT DRIVES.

To **High Bridge**, via Bloomingdale.—Proceed north in Broadway, through Bloomingdale road, into the Ninth avenue.

To **High Bridge**, via McComb's Dam.—Proceed north in Broadway to No. 948, and north in Fifth avenue to Harlem River; after crossing the river, proceed west.

To **Fort Washington**.—Proceed north in Broadway, through Bloomingdale, Manhattanville and Carmansville, along the King's Bridge road to 175th street, and west to the river.

To **Jamaica**, via Cypress Hills' Cemetery.—Proceed to No. 458 Broadway, east in Grand street to the river, cross Division avenue ferry; pass through South 7th and South 6th streets and Broadway, east into Johnson street, which leads to the plank road.

To **Flushing**, via Green Point and Newtown.—Proceed in Broadway to No. 784, and east in Tenth street to the river; cross the ferry, and proceed east along the plank road.

To **Paterson**, via Hoboken.—Proceed to either No. 227, 417, or 769 Broadway, and west through Barclay, Canal, or Ninth and Christopher streets to the river, and cross the ferry—taking the plank road to the west.

OBJECTS OF INTEREST.

High Bridge, (over Harlem River.)—Drive out Broadway and Bloomingdale road, and into the 9th avenue beyond Bloomingdale—or take a car to Harlem, from 4th avenue and 27th street, and then take stages west from Harlem. (See engraving.)

Distributing Reservoir, (5th avenue and 42d street.)—Take a Broadway and 42d street, or a 5th avenue stage, or a 6th avenue car from Broadway and Vesey or Canal street, to 42d street.

Receiving Reservoir, (86th street.)—Take a 2d, 3d or 4th avenue car to 86th street, and proceed west.

Greenwood Cemetery, (South Brooklyn.)—Proceed to 208 Broadway, and east in Fulton street to the East River; cross the ferry, and take the Court street cars, which go to the Cemetery gate.

Hoboken and Elysian Fields.—Proceed to either 227, 417, or 769 Broadway, and west through Barclay, Canal, or Ninth and Christopher streets to the river, and cross the ferry.

HOW TO LEAVE NEW YORK.

For **Philadelphia**, via New Jersey Railroad Depot at Jersey City.—Proceed to 171 Broadway, thence to the foot of Courtlandt street, and cross the ferry.

For **Philadelphia**, via Camden and Amboy Railroad.—From Pier No. 1 North River. Proceed to No. 1 Broadway, and west in Battery Place to the river.

For **Boston**, via Stonington and Providence.—From Pier No. 2 North River. Proceed to No. 1 Broadway, and west through Battery Place to the river.

For **Boston**, via Fall River and Newport.—From Pier No. 3 North River. Proceed to No. 1 Broadway, and west through Battery Place to the river.

For **Boston**, via Norwich and Worcester.—From foot of Courtlandt street. Proceed to No. 171 Broadway, and thence through Courtlandt street to the river.

For **Boston**, via New Haven Railroad.—Depot 27th street and 4th avenue. Take a 4th avenue car, which starts from the Astor House, or a Broadway and 4th avenue stage, north to 27th street.

For **Albany**, via Hudson River Railroad.—Depot, Warren street and College Place. Proceed to 260 Broadway, and west in Warren street to College Place.

For **Albany**, via Harlem Railroad.—Depot 27th street, corner 4th avenue. Take a 4th avenue car, which starts from the Astor House, or a Broadway and 4th avenue stage, north to 27th street.

For **Albany**, via People's Line Steamboats.—From foot of Courtlandt street. Proceed in Broadway to No. 171, and west in Courtlandt street to the river.

For **Albany**, via Merchants' Line Steamboats.—From foot of Robinson street. Proceed to No. 237 Broadway, and through Park Place west to the river.

For **Buffalo or Dunkirk**, via New York and Erie Railroad.—Depot, foot of Duane street. Proceed in Broadway to No. 303, and west in Duane street to the river.

For **New Haven**, by steamboat.—From Peck Slip. Proceed to 208 Broadway, and east in Fulton street to the river; thence northeast two blocks.

HIGH BRIDGE, CROTON AQUEDUCT.

Among the gigantic enterprises of modern times, the magnificent Croton Aqueduct, which supplies the City of New York with a never-failing stream of pure water, may justly be considered as the finest, both as to cost, and to the magnitude of its public uses. Through this immense structure, water is conveyed to the city, from Croton River, over 40 miles distant. The dam on Croton River is 40 feet high, and 166 feet above tide water. Through a covered canal strongly built of brick and stone, and 16 tunnels of an aggregate length of 6841 feet, the water is conveyed to Harlem River, which it crosses on the High Bridge, represented in the above engraving. This bridge is 1450 feet long, and is supported by 8 arches, with a span of 80 feet each, springing from piers 20 feet wide, the upper structure being 114 feet above the river.

About five miles above the City Hall is the receiving reservoir, covering 38 acres, and capable of holding 150,000,000 gallons of water.

Near 3 miles below, on Fifth Avenue, is the distributing reservoir, which has a capacity of 20,000,000 gallons. In supplying the city from this point, some 300 miles of pipe have been laid, capable of distributing 60,000,000 of gallons daily. The whole works, in connection with bringing the water into the city, has cost upwards of $15,000,000 (£2,400,000 stg).

During the Summer months, "High Bridge" is much visited, the scenery around being very charming, and the river at this point being favorable for fishing purposes. This Spring (1859) a line of small steamers have commenced running every hour, from Peck Slip to High Bridge, at the small fare of 16 cents each way.

GREENWOOD CEMETERY.

This beautiful enclosure occupies an area of 400 acres, and is the most extensive place of sepulture ever formed in modern times. Here Nature and Art have combined to produce all the quiet and graceful surroundings which the most affectionate heart could desire for the last resting-place of its beloved ones. One can scarcely imagine a form of scenic beauty that cannot be found in this mournful, but enchanting place. Apart from its sad uses, it might well be mistaken for an earthly paradise. Hills, valleys, and plains; strips of woodland and a series of brush enclosures, with here and there a tiny lake, whose placid bosom sparkles with silver light, are met with in constant succession by the visitors who thread the silent avenues of this "City of the Dead." A whole day is not too much to devote to a thorough review of these grounds, and the various interesting monuments, which are to be met with on every hand. An hour's ride will only allow of a circuit around the enclosure, without offering opportunity for any thing like a fair inspection of the most notable points of interest. Strangers or citizens desirous of visiting this Cemetery, which is by far the most interesting place of the kind in the country, can procure free tickets of admission by calling at the company's office at No. 30 Broadway, New York. The Cemetery is reached from New York, by crossing on Fulton Ferry to Brooklyn, where a line of horse cars is always ready to take passengers on the landing of each boat, direct to the grounds, at a fare of 5 cents each person. Carriages are in attendance at the Cemetery gate, for the accommodation of such visitors as prefer to ride

BROOKLYN, NEW YORK.

The City of Brooklyn is justly considered one of the most delightful places in the Union. Its close proximity to New York, its beautiful, cleanly and well-shaded streets, its salubrious atmosphere, the reputation of its divines and professional men, and the general elevated character and public spirit of its citizens, all combine to give to this "City of Churches" advantages which, if we may judge from the remarkably rapid growth of its population, do not fail of appreciation. Brooklyn, as now consolidated, numbers 225,000 inhabitants, and is therefore the third city in point of population in the United States.

Several lines of steam ferries run from the principal thoroughfares of the city, and connect with various points on the New York side, boats starting every two or three minutes, the fares being from one to three cents for each passenger. From most of these ferries city railways diverge in every direction into the country, which give to the city great freedom and capacity for expansion and growth.

Brooklyn is one of the best built cities in the United States. Its site is considerably elevated, that prominent portion known as the "Heights" being 70 feet above the river, and affording a most magnificent view of New York, the harbour and the surrounding country. The streets, with but one or two exceptions, are straight and even, intersecting each other at right angles, and being generally of about 60 feet in width. Many of these streets, especially those lying on the south-west side of the city, are adorned with elegant and substantial private residences, surrounded by fine yards and tastefully-arranged gardens, while long lines of magnificent trees stretch on either side as far as the eye can reach, giving a lovely rural appearance to the city, which is really delightful, especially during the summer season.

Brooklyn was first settled in 1625. In 1806 it was incorporated as a township, and in 1834 received a city charter. In January, 1855, by a legislative act, Brooklyn, Williamsburgh and Bushwick were consolidated into one city, which has been divided into eighteen wards, each one forming a township in King's County.

The public buildings of Brooklyn are numerous, and many of them are elegant and imposing structures. It numbers over seventy houses of Christian worship, which has given it the title of "The City of Churches."

Among the public charitable institutions, we may mention the City Hospital, which has accommodations for 175 patients; the Graham Institution, for the relief of aged and indigent females, with room for nearly 100 persons; the Orphan Asylum, which furnishes a home for 200 children; the Marine Hospital, for sailors, and several other smaller charities.

The principal literary institutions are the Brooklyn Athenæum, which contains a free library, a reading-room, and a large hall for lectures, and was erected at a cost of $60,000; the City Library, containing a large number of valuable books; the Lyceum, a fine granite building, with a large lecture-room, and the United States Lyceum, which is situated in the Navy Yard, and contains a rare collection of curiosities, including geological and mineralogical cabinets.

The United States Navy Yard occupies forty acres of ground on the south side of Wallabout Bay, and is well worth visiting by strangers, who are readily admitted on application at the gates.

The Atlantic Dock is also worthy of note as being one of the most extensive works of the kind in the country. It was erected in 1840, at an expense of $1,000,000, and is of sufficient depth to accommodate ships of the largest class.

Quite a large number of fine buildings have been erected for educational purposes, among the finest of which are the Polytechnic Institute for the education of boys, now numbering between 400 and 500 pupils, and the Packer Institute for young ladies, having over 700 pupils.

Among the great improvements of this year, (1859,) the most important is the introduction of pure water into the city, which will add largely to the health, wealth, and growth of the population.

Some of the finest cemeteries on the continent are located in Brooklyn. The most noted of these are Greenwood, the Evergreens, Cypress Hills, and Calvary Cemeteries. A brief description of the first-mentioned will be found on the preceding page.

COMPARATIVE

TIME INDICATOR.

COMPARATIVE TIME INDICATOR,

Showing the Time at the Principal Cities of the United States and Canada, compared with Noon at Washington, New York and Montreal.

There is no standard railroad time in America as in Great Britain. Each railroad company adopts the time of its own locality.

Travellers are apt to experience considerable annoyance in consequence of such difference. The only way is to observe what difference there is between the time in each particular place, and arrange accordingly.

For difference of time between Washington and the chief cities in the United States and Canada, see Time Indicator on following page:—

NOON AT NEW YORK. At	It will be	NOON AT MONTREAL. At	It will be
Augusta, Ga	11 30 A. M.	Boston	12 12 P. M.
Baltimore, Md.	11 50 "	Buffalo	11 40 A. M.
Boston	12 12 P. M.	Collingwood, C. W	11 33 "
Buffalo, N. Y	11 40 A. M.	Goderich, C. W	11 28 "
Charleston, S. C.	11 36 "	Hamilton, C. W	11 35 "
Chicago, Ill.	11 6 "	Kingston, C. W.	11 49 "
Cincinnati, O.	11 18 "	London, C. W	11 30 "
Cleveland, O.	11 30 "	New York City	11 58 "
Columbus, O.	11 24 "	Ottawa, C. W	11 52 "
Detroit, Mich	11 24 "	Paris, C. W	11 37 "
Indianapolis, Ind.	11 14 "	Peterborough, C. W	11 40 "
Louisville, Ky	11 14 "	Port Hope, C. W	11 40 "
New Orleans, La.	10 54 "	Portland, Me.	12 14 P. M.
Philadelphia	11 55 "	Quebec, C. E.	12 10 "
Pittsburg, Pa.	11 35 "	Richmond	12 6 "
Portland, Me.	12 16 "	Sarnia, C. W	11 25 A. M.
Richmond, Va.	11 46 "	St. Thomas, C. E.	12 13 "
St. Louis, Mo	10 55 "	Three Rivers, C. E	12 4 P. M.
St. Paul, Min.	10 45 "	Toronto, C. W.	11 36 "
		Windsor, C. W	11 23 A. M.

DIFFERENCE OF TIME BETWEEN EUROPE AND AMERICA.

WHEN IT IS NOON AT NEW YORK,

At	It will be	At	It will be
London	4 55 P. M.	Madrid	4 40 P. M.
Liverpool	4 44 "	Rome	5 46 "
Dublin	4 30 "	Hamburg	5 35 "
Edinburgh	4 43 "	Constantinople	6 51 "
Glasgow	4 44 "	Paris	"

GAMBLING ON THE RIVER.

Some five-and-twenty years ago, gambling was as prevalent on the Western rivers as eating, drinking, or even conversation. Just as soon as breakfast, dinner, or supper was ended, the tables were cleared for card-playing, which was indulged in until preparations for the next meal disturbed the sport. Gamblers, in pairs, sixes, and sometimes in dozens, were found on board every boat. These harpies did nothing else but traverse the rivers, up on one boat and down on another, fleecing and bullying the passengers with impunity. The general rendezvous of these rogues were on points below Memphis, on the Mississippi; especially at Vicksburg and Natchez. At these places, the gamblers seemed determined to overawe the citizens, by their brutality and arrogance. They strutted through the streets, occupied the best rooms in the hotels, and in various other ways elbowed the honest merchant and mechanic, with an impudence bordering almost on the sublime. These things were borne, until forbearance ceased to be a virtue; when, one morning, the gamblers of Vicksburg were waited upon by a company of determined citizens, and ordered to leave the town forthwith, on peril of their lives. The more timid of the gamblers showed their discretion by retreat; but some of the hardened ones, who had grown over-bold from former successes, remained over the time specified. The citizens, not wishing to shed blood, if it could be avoided, gave a further period to the day of grace, which the gamblers paid no attention to. The enraged citizens, goaded beyond the bounds of reason, by the recollection of the gamblers' former acts, as well as by their present wilful arrogance, seized upon some of the most noted of their number, and hanged them in the streets of the city. The citizens of Natchez followed suit, and strung up a few of their gamblers; and, the fire of reform spreading up and down the rivers with astonishing rapidity, soon had the effect of banishing from the South—for the time being, at least—some of the worst gangs of gamblers that ever infested any country. They dispersed in various directions, some going to New Orleans and others turning towards the North, and it was, for a long while, dangerous for known "blacklegs" to be seen on a Western steamer. But we are sorry to say that, of late, there seems to be indications of a return to the old customs; and the steamers of the North, as well as of the South and West, are sometimes disgraced by the presence of professed gamblers, who, as a general rule, are never over-scrupulous how they get the passengers' money—whether by *cards, dice,* or *light fingers.* Of course, our remarks do not apply to an innocent game of cards, between friends, for mere amusement's sake. We mean, the combination of two or more gamblers, who seduce a verdant passenger into taking a "third," or "fourth," in some cut-throat game, in which he is "dead-sure" to be beaten. We advise all travellers to beware of such *apparent* gentlemen—for gamblers are proverbially well-dressed and gentlemanly in external deportment—and to refuse "making up a party" with persons with whom they are unacquainted.

We have been induced to write this article of warning, by reading a paragraph in the *New York Herald,* of the day on which this is written, which we insert here for the benefit of our travelling friends.

"GAMBLING ON THE NORTH RIVER STEAMBOATS.—Since the opening of navigation on the Hudson river, the steamboats plying between this city and Albany have been besieged, in their trips to and from this city, by parties of fashionably dressed gamblers, who, it is said, have been doing an extensive business among verdant travellers. A gentleman, our informant, who came down on one of the boats a few nights ago, related the following instance which came under his own observation, and which is but one, probably, of many similar cases:—It appears that an Englishman, who had amassed considerable money in agricultural pursuits in the West, was on the boat, in company with his wife and six children, *in transitu* for England. Shortly after the boat left Albany, he became acquainted with a very gentlemanly-appearing man, who, after a brief conversation, invited him to take some "refreshment" at the bar. The invitation was accepted. In a few minutes, the potation which the Western man had taken made him feel unusually lively. The gambler—for that was his confronter's true character—then proposed to play a game of cards, which was assented to, and both parties repaired to the 'card-room'—an apartment fitted up expressly for the purpose. In this room the *quasi* friend was joined by others of the same kin, and in a few minutes the party was engaged in playing "three-card monte." In less than one hour, the Western man was fleeced of almost every dollar he possessed—over one thousand dollars. As soon as he had recovered from the effects of the stupefying draught he had taken, and saw his true condition, without scarcely a dollar in the world, he was seized with a fit of frenzy, and threatened self-destruction. In his agony of mind, in pacing up and down the steamer's deck, he represented his case to a party of gentlemen, who resolved themselves into a Vigilance Committee, and proceeded at once to the room occupied by the gamblers. The gentlemen, in the most summary manner, demanded immediate restoration of their ill-gotten gain to its rightful owner. The gamblers were intimidated, and every dollar was given back to the Western man. The scene that ensued, when the poor fellow got back his money, can be better imagined than described.

"It cannot be believed, for a moment, that such acts as the above are tolerated by the owners of our North River palaces; yet the statement above, is a faithful statement of the facts in the case."

BETWEEN

NEW YORK AND BOSTON,

Via Newport and Fall River.

THE

New York, Boston & Fall River Line,

BY THE SPLENDID AND SUPERIOR STEAMERS

METROPOLIS, BAY STATE AND EMPIRE STATE,

Of great strength and speed, particularly adapted to the navigation of Long Island Sound, running in connection with the

FALL RIVER AND OLD COLONY RAILROADS,

a distance of fifty-three miles only of railroad to Boston.

Leave New York, from Pier No. 3, North River, near the Battery,

The Steamer METROPOLIS, Captain Brown,

on Tuesdays, Thursdays, and Saturdays, at 5 o'clock P. M. in the Summer, and 4 P. M. in the Winter, touching at Newport each way.

The Steamer EMPIRE STATE, Capt. Brayton,

on Mondays, Wednesdays and Fridays, at 5 o'clock P. M. in the Summer, and 4 P. M. in the Winter, touching at Newport each way.

The Steamer BAY STATE, Captain Jewett.

A Train of Cars, to connect with these Boats at Fall River for New York, leaves Boston every afternoon from the Depot of the Old Colony and Fall River Railroad.

The Steamers of this Line are fitted with commodious state-rooms, and every arrangement for the security and comfort of passengers, who are afforded by this route a night's rest on board, and on arrival at Fall River, proceed per railroad again, reaching Boston early on the following morning.

A baggage master is attached to each steamer, who receives and tickets the baggage, and accompanies the same to its destination.

A steamer runs in connection with this line, between Fall River and Providence, daily, except Sundays.

Freight to Boston is taken at the same rates as by other regular lines, and forwarded with the greatest expedition, by an Express freight train, which leaves Fall River every morning (Sundays excepted), at 7¼ o'clock, for Boston and New Bedford, arriving at its destination at about 11 o'clock A. M.

For freight or passage apply on board, or at the office on Pier 3, North River, where state-rooms and berths may be secured. Hereafter no rooms will be regarded as secured to any applicant until the same shall have been paid for. For further information apply to

WM. BORDEN,

70 and 71 West Street, N. Y.

ALEX. HARTHILL & Co., *Steam Printers*, 20 *North William St., New York.*

ROUND HILL WATER CURE AND HOTEL,

AT NORTHAMPTON, MASS.

H. HALSTED, M. D., Proprietor.

"SUMMER RESORT.—It is not every one who, though desirous of getting out of the city, wishes to spend the summer months at a hotel. To such, therefore, we would call attention to a very charming place of resort at Northampton, Massachusetts, We refer to the 'Round Hill' establishment, under the control of Dr. H. Halsted. Here Nature is clothed in her most attractive garb; and woods, glens, brooks, and flowers, each contributes its part to make Round Hill a delightful spot for all, whether invalids seeking health, or the convalescent searching for pleasure."—*Home Journal.*

☞ SEE CIRCULAR, SENT GRATIS.

NORTHAMPTON COLLEGIATE INSTITUTE.

This is a Family School for boys, in Northampton, Mass. A place of many attractions and few temptations. A genial home, provident care, and the best of tuition are furnished. The number of pupils is limited. They are under the personal supervision and instruction of the Principal. In sickness, as well as in health, a mother's place is supplied by the wife of the Principal. Pupils are prepared for college or for business. The Principal was, for six years, a Tutor in Yale College, and has had nineteen years' experience as a teacher. The School has been patronized by families of the highest social position in almost every State in the Union. Reference is made to the following patrons:

Philadelphia—J. Pemberton Hutchinson, F. A. Packard. *York, Pa.*—Hon. R. J. Fisher. *Harrisburg, Pa.*—John A. Fisher. *Elmira, N. Y.*—John Arnat. *Rochester, N. Y.*—Hon. Samuel Miller. *New York City*—Hon. Lewis B. Woodruff, Robert Ray, Henry F. Vail, James M'Call, M. O. Roberts, Frederick Prime, Nathan Smith, L. Tuckerman.

Catalogues may be had of the Principal.

LEWIS J. DUDLEY.

CARRIAGE MANUFACTORY OF G. & D. COOK, NEW HAVEN, CONN.

CARRIAGE MANUFACTURING.

No branch of business with which we are conversant, has more rapidly developed itself in the last twenty years, or attained higher rank among the great manufacturing interests of the country, than that indicated in the heading of this article.

Twenty years ago, the farmer or mechanic would have considered the keeping of a pleasure carriage an unwarrantable extravagance; those who were obliged to have some kind of a vehicle could afford nothing better than the square box-waggon, set flat upon rough wooden axles, and in many instances with no other seat than a board thrown across the top of the body; and this must be used upon all occasions, and for all purposes, whether to carry the family to meeting, the grist to the mill, or the pork and poultry to market. But gradually, as the facilities for the manufacture of carriages have increased, thereby lessening their cost, this state of things has undergone a wonderful change, and to-day the thriving mechanic and the well-to-do farmer must have, in addition to his genteel, tastefully-painted business-waggon, with iron axles, steel springs and cushioned seat, a fine top buggy, rockaway, or couch; in short, a pleasure waggon of some kind has become indispensable.

From among the many carriage manufacturers whose success has tended to produce this great change, we select one to illustrate our subject.

Above we give a partial view of the premises of Messrs. G. and D. Cook & Co., New Haven, Conn. This firm commenced business about nine years since, in a small shop, at the corner of Grove and State streets, New Haven, where their present large and commodious establishment now stands. At the commencement of their business they adopted a principle entirely novel among carriage-makers, viz.: that of systematizing, dividing, and sub-dividing their work in such a manner that each man had but a single part to perform, thereby enabling him to learn it to such perfection that he could execute it very rapidly and at a great reduction of cost. One can readily conceive of the advantage this system would give them over their competitors who performed their work after the old plan—each man performing all the different parts in turn until the carriage was completed. The successful operation of their system enabled them to turn out one carriage per day, which at that time was considered a wonderful achievement, and soon attracted the general attention of the craft. This well known firm now complete, by the same system, no less than *ten per day*, with the same ease and success with which they could then complete one per day. Their original factory was a single building, fifty feet by twenty feet, two stories in height, giving them with the basement about 3,000 square feet of floor-room, which has since increased to the immense proportions shown in the picture, increasing their floor-room from 3,000 to over 85,000 square feet, equal to a one-story building covering *two acres* of ground. This establishment now gives employment to over three hundred workmen, and in addition to this force they have a beautiful and powerful steam-engine, every revolution of whose ponderous wheel gives life and activity to over fifty beautifully working machines, adapted to almost any conceivable part of their work, performing an amount of work equal to the whole number of their men, and with far greater accuracy than can possibly be done by hand labor. When we look at the powerful array of forces we no longer wonder that their elegant pleasure wagons are completed at the rate of one per hour, and even then not keeping pace with their orders, which their liberal advertisements, scattered broadcast over the land in the form of newspapers, books, charts, descriptive catalogues, etc., have brought them from almost all parts of the habitable globe where carriage wheels have rolled, making the name of G. & D. Cook & Co., not only in New Haven, but in every city in the Union, as "familiar as household words."

Should you visit the establishment of the Messrs. Cook, you will always find one of their firm ready to attend to your wants and to conduct you through all the departments of their mammoth factory, explaining the operations of the numerous machines, from the delicate sewing machine (of which they have some dozen in the trimming department), to the huge monster who stands near the entrance to the basement, puffing from his powerful iron lungs the breath which keeps alive the numerous forge fires in their immense blacksmith's shop.

Their cordial and gentlemanly bearing towards all visitors and customers is highly appreciated, and the liberal course they have ever pursued, together with the taste, skill, and talent manifested in all their operations, have made the firm the well known favorite of the carriage-dealers and consumers throughout the country.—*Life Illustrated.*

www.ingramcontent.com/pod-product-compliance
Lightning Source LLC
Chambersburg PA
CBHW020226090426
42735CB00010B/1596

* 9 7 8 3 3 3 7 3 0 1 5 4 5 *